RIVER RAMBLINGS & FLOA

RECOLLECTIONS AND RECIPES

by the
Memphis Yacht Club
Celebrating 110 Years

EDITED AND DESIGNED BY NOAH TOWERY
RECIPES EDITED BY ARDITH BRADSHAW
RECIPE SECTION DESIGNED BY BOB TOWERY

Library of Congress Control Number: 2012900055
by the Memphis Yacht Club founded 1959
RIVER RAMBLINGS AND FLOATING FARE—RECOLLECTIONS AND RECIPES
documents the Memphis Yacht Club's colorful history, and presents its
favorite shipboard cuisine.

PHOTO OF THE JACK RATHBONE COURTESY OF BOB SCHWARTZ

Contents

RECIPES

Featuring contributions from Kay Bolgeo, Anne Brown, Charles Cook, Pat Hill, Donald Manker, and others…

Beginnings

At the crux of Memphis and the Mississippi River sits the Memphis Yacht Club. For over one hundred years the club has witnessed and played a part in the history of the river and the city. As such, no telling of its story would be complete without the larger context of the developments of life in Memphis and on the Mississippi. A friend to neighbors and passing strangers alike, the club has always provided an oasis for travelers while cultivating a culture of respect for the river and one another. Every member has a story to tell, and as with any long-lived organization, those experiences and recollections overrun the historical record.

As far as it is known, the predecessors of the yacht club were informal canoeing clubs. Long-time member Ham Smythe recalls his own father's tales of that early period, saying that they would go out in their canoes to ride the wakes of the paddle boats. As the paddle wheels churned the water, they created massive waves, acting like white water rapids for those undaunted thrill-seekers in canoes.

Eventually the popularity of pleasure boating gave rise to the Memphis Boat Club, as the Memphis Yacht Club was originally known. The first mention of the Memphis Boat Club is a short paragraph in the "River News" section of the Commercial Appeal dated February 23rd, 1901. Under the sub-header "That Boating Club" comes the following: "The river men are now interested in the boating club. The contract for the construction of the floating boathouse has been let and it will be one of the most complete ever launched on the Mississippi river." One of the members of the club told the paper that they would complete the building of their new home by the first of April. The house would be made of longleaf yellow pine, 110 feet long with a 24-foot hull. The first story would be occupied by a dance hall, with rooms and lockers for members on the second floor. There would also be a landing dock with a 34-foot beam attached to the new clubhouse "so that there will be no trouble about steamers 'making fast' when an excursion party is on." The reporter concluded, "The members are determined to make the club a success."

PAGE RIGHT: A VIEW OF THE MEMPHIS RIVERSIDE FROM 1903.

COURTESY OF THE MEMPHIS AND SHELBY COUNTY ROOM, MEMPHIS PUBLIC LIBRARY & INFORMATION CENTER

MYC

Memphis Boat Club.

POST CARD

MEMPHIS
1 PM
1908

Germany

PCH
SERIES

S.A. Burmeister Jr.
1153-18 St.

The foundation of the club came at a time when Memphis was beginning to experience strong growth, but still recovering from the devastating yellow fever epidemics of the late 19th century. At the same time as the club was sketching plans and buying timber for their floating clubhouse, other renovations and expansions were underway along the riverfront. Memphis was at that time the largest hardwood lumber market in the world, and the largest inland market for cotton. Business was limited only by the availability of landing room on the riverbank. In February of 1901 the Mississippi reached one of its lowest levels in years, causing Memphians to consider paving more of the sandbank. A local engineer described the riverfront this way:

As the case stands, the bar can only be utilized for unloading lumber and other stuff that is floated into the harbor on barges, but there is no reason in the world why all that space should not be utilized by the regular packets…We will certainly need more room during the coming busy season than we have ever needed, because the river business of this port is expanding just as well as every other class of business that the city is doing is expanding.[1]

---

1.   *The Commercial Appeal*, 2/22/01.

MYC

It was suggested that the paving of the bank be expanded up to the foot of Jefferson Street, which was right around where the new clubhouse was being built.

It was announced on Monday morning, March 25, 1901 in the Commercial Appeal that building of the clubhouse would begin immediately. It would be located in the waters at the foot of Court Street. The paper had this to say about the club's rising popularity: "Few of the many clubs which have been organized in this city can boast of the immediate success which has greeted the Memphis Boat Club. Its quick popularity has fairly surprised even Will E. Gage and other young gentlemen who projected the idea." The article goes on to note that the organization of the club had taken place about six months ago, placing the original founding date sometime in the autumn of 1900. However, research has failed to uncover any references to the club earlier than February of 1901.

At the time of its founding, membership in the Boat Club was limited to 150, and by March 25, 1901 there were already 142 members. With just eight vacancies remaining and about 175 applications, "the permanence and prosperity of the club [were], therefore, assured." The initiation fee was $25 and semi-annual dues of $9

MEMPHIS BOAT CLUB

FLATTERING SUCCESS WHICH HAS ATTENDED ITS ORGANIZATION.

HOUSE TO BE BUILT AT ONCE

Work Will Begin This Week on the Elaborate Structure Which Will Be Launched With an Elegant Social Function.

helped support expenses for the club, whose stated purpose was "social enjoyment with aquatic recreations."

An account of the club's first annual meeting appears in the Wednesday, February 11th, 1902 edition of the Commercial Appeal, with a summary of the minutes:

Twenty odd members participated in the annual meeting and smoker of the Memphis Boat Club last night at the office of W.A. Gage & Co. Several amendments to the constitution were made, a new board of directors was elected and plans and arrangements discussed for a regatta and athletic meeting next May. By means of proxies a quorum of thirty-five was obtained. It was regretted by those present that a larger attendance was not on hand, though this was attributable to the fact that there were several entertainments last night.

PAGE LEFT: THE ANNOUNCEMENT OF THE BUILDING OF THE CLUBHOUSE, PUBLISHED IN THE COMMERCIAL APPEAL ON MARCH 25, 1901.

Here and in other early accounts of the club, W. A. Gage and W. E. Gage[2] are mentioned as founding members. W. A. Gage served as president of the Memphis Cotton Exchange from 1900-1901. The meeting began like this:

The first business taken up was the report of the secretary, which was read and adopted. The report of the treasurer, W.H. Smith,

2   W.E. Gage also started the Marine Supply Company, run today (2012) by his grandson, **Andy Cole**.

which followed, showed the financial condition of the club was very good, considering that it was in the first year of its existence.

W. H. Smith went on to discuss the finances of the club whose receipts for the year ending February 1, 1902, were $6,458.22. The assets of the club at that early period consisted of the boat house, valued at $3,548.85, boats valued at $470.90, and incidentals of $80.25. The assets of the club were owned by 127 shares of stock, the face value of which was $3,175, making the book value of stock at the time $111. The article continues,

The sentiment of the club over this report was that it was to be congratulated on such a good showing for the first year. It was also developed that the membership was 125 from a total of 137 a year ago, twelve having dropped out. The membership is limited to 150 and it is expected that this will be filled by spring.

Next on the docket was the question of delinquent dues. The club decided that members who were two months late would be put on notice. If they failed to pay within a week's time, they would be dropped, with their stock going to the benefit of the club. With that resolved, the members delved into a "spirited discussion" of the age of admittance to the club:

It was proposed to change this from 18 years to 16. The argument was advanced, however, that this would seem like cheapening the privilege by bidding for boys, also that the step might prove dangerous in youths so young. The motion was finally tabled, it being thought best to let the board of directors act separately upon each application.

Apparently the board of directors was having problems with attendance, so it was adopted that any director who missed three consecutive meetings would forfeit his membership on the board, and a new director would be elected. One member suggested that "the only way to get directors to attend any sort of meetings was to pay them and then you could not keep them away." This was followed by the election of the directors for the following year. They were E. T. McHenry, C. S. Williams, W. H. Kyle, R. W. Lake, B. Smith, H. J. McKenzie, W. H. Smith, W. E. Gage, J. S. Warren, and J. A. Reichman. With the amendments made and the board elected, they went on to planning events:

The rest of the evening was devoted to a discussion of the best means of promoting a regatta in the spring. On motion, the president appointed a committee consisting of Messrs. McHenry, McKenzie and McKinney to arrange the details and various classes for the meeting.

It was decided to hold it in the latter part of May in order that there might be sufficient time for training.

Considerable enthusiasm was displayed by the members in this affair and the entries which will include sailing, rowing and swimming contests, as well as other forms of athletic sports, will be many. A tub race is among those contemplated and if engaged in will be the first one held in these waters. The races will be handicapped so that everyone may have a chance for the handsome prizes which will be offered.

T he Memphis Boat Club's next mention in the historical record came in April of 1902, about month before their first spring regatta. Evidently they had finished building their clubhouse, because the members had decorated it in anticipation of welcoming a famous naval hero, Admiral Winfield Scott Schley. America had recently concluded its 1898 war with Spain, and in Washington there was ongoing debate about the fate of the colonies of Cuba and the Philippines. Although he was reprimanded by the Navy for reckless conduct, Admiral Schley was being hailed as a hero across the country for his part in the decisive naval victory over the Spanish fleet at Santiago, Cuba. Touring the country

1923

MEMPHIS

Population 190,000
(Estimate by R. L. Polk, Publishers, in 1923 City Directory)
Immediate Suburbs....... 40,000

by steamboat to thunderous applause, he arrived in Memphis to a lavish welcome.

The Commercial Appeal ran the headline, "Great Day for Schley," and described the festivities of the welcoming party, including the participation of the Memphis Boat Club. The steamboats Robert E. Lee, the Delta, and the Georgia Lee accompanied the Admiral's vessel in a parade, their riggings hung with bunting and decked with flags. After a warm reception speech given by Memphis Mayor J. J. Williams, Schley went on to meet the members of the boat club.

When the Admiral's party arrived, they were met at the stage plank by "a special committee of the Memphis Boat Club. This committee was composed of J. A. Reichman, president; J. A. Sylvester, W. P. Metcalf, E. B. McHenry, and W. H. Kyle." The men "escorted the admiral's party to the end of the wharf boat and thence on board the floating clubhouse of the Memphis Boat Club."

Once all were aboard the floating clubhouse, W. P. Metcalf offered this welcome on behalf of the club:

Admiral Schley, I have the honor and pleasure on behalf of the members of the Memphis Boat Club of extending to you a most cordial welcome and an assurance equally sincere of the high esteem entertained for your noble character and heroic services.

I but echo the language of the throng which has crowded around you, in saying that the frank and manly simplicity of your character has created a feeling of friendship and personal regard for you which the glory of your noble naval achievement alone could not have secured.

Feel the assurance of the universal recognition among the members of this club to your claim for admiration, while we feel the honor of your presence among us.[1]

Metcalf's speech of great admiration was followed by a reception on board, the members and their lady friends having gone to great trouble to make the admiral's stay pleasant: "In decorating the clubhouse the members had spared no expense. The upper decks were draped in flags and the interior was made bright with bunting

MYC

---

1   *The Commercial Appeal* 4/30/1902

and flowers."[2] The members must have felt proud indeed that day welcoming a hero of war aboard their newly minted clubhouse.

By May, things were stepping into high gear for the organization of the spring regatta. On the 25th an announcement was made in the paper with the headlines, "BOAT CLUB REGATTA: ALL WATER SPORTS INCLUDED." The date of the regatta was set for the 30th, entries having been closed the previous day. But the city hardly needed to be reminded of the date, as enthusiasm had been growing since the plans were laid out in February. The list of contestants had grown steadily over the past month, as the river had been "dotted with the craft of the M.B.C. almost every afternoon."

In charge of organizing the event were the officers of the club: J. A. Riechman, commodore; Edgar T. McHenry, vice-commodore; C. S. Williams, rear commodore; Bolton Smith, fleet captain; Dr. Richmond McKinney, fleet surgeon; and Wright Smith, secretary and treasurer. The planners took care to include an array of events, "affording every kind of a boat a chance for the handsome prizes which are to be given to the firsts over the line." With the recent surge in membership, the M.B.C.'s fleet now included "some fliers of

---

2   *The Commercial Appeal* 5/25/1902

the first-class order, both in sailing and launches." And with a little help from the wind, everyone expected some of the fastest racing ever witnessed on the Mississippi.

The races were set to begin at 3 o'clock in the afternoon on the 30th of May, 1902. The full regatta would consist of ten events, including sailboat racing and walking a greased spar.

Here is the description of the race course: "The course will be one of four legs –nautical ones. It starts from the club boathouse [at the foot of Court St.] and goes north to the mouth of the Wolf River and around a buoy just off the bar on the Tennessee side and across to Hopefield on the Arkansas side. The last leg is then the stretch back to the club boat."[3] Dr. Richmond McKinney would start the event, and George James would referee. The judges were A. D. Gibson, Jr., Bolton Smith, and W. M. Goodbar.

On the day of the race the paper announced: "The excitement and interest is intense, having grown to a climax from the days of hard exercising and preliminary work by the members." The event ran from 1 o'clock to 7, "on the broad bosom of the Father of Waters." The start and finish line was at the clubhouse

3   *The Commercial Appeal* 5/30/1902

at the foot of Court Street. There spectators gathered to view "the contests of skill, brains, and daring." They looked on at the "maneuvers of the bold young masters of the watery deep." Ready in case of emergency, safety boats with life preservers followed in the wake of the canoe, skiff, tub, scull, and paddling races. In addition to the boat races, the M.B.C. promised a "cold bottle as a trophy for the contestant who can walk a greased spar."

The main event was a free-for-all sailing race on five mile course, starting and finishing at the boathouse. As for the grand prize, George T. Brodnax donated a "handsome silver cup," which was currently "on exhibition in Brodnax's window on Main Street."[4] Seven contestants vied for the prize. The boats and their captains were the following:

Swallow	W. E. Gage
Skylark	Wm. H. Carrol, Jr.
Mudlark	H. S. Hayley
Highflyer	Horace Smith
Alice Clare	W. O. Whitaker
Louise	Percy Galbreath
Folly	P. S. Coole

---

4   The Broadnax building still stands, and is presently (2012) home to Flight Restaurant and Wine Bar.

Just after 1 o'clock the boats gathered at the starting line. After the starting gun, "The boats got under way in good shape and immediately after they had proceeded a short distance broke out their spinnakers, which materially aided them through the water at racing pace…It was an evenly matched affair under the conditions imposed by the handicapper and the result was in doubt until the last stakeboat was turned." The Louise crossed the finish line first, followed by the Highflyer and then the Swallow.[5]

The several other contests followed to fill the rest of the afternoon, and it was agreed upon by all involved to be a great success. The tub race, however, failed to materialize, and "there were no aspirants for honors in the greased spar contest." The paper made this conclusion about the Memphis Boat Club that day: "Each member takes an individual pride both in the work of the association and the clubhouse furnishings and the combination of interests has given Memphis a boating association second to none in the country."[6]

The members of this early era of the club have of course long since passed on, and with them their memories and stories of how things once were. What is most astonishing about the

PAGE RIGHT: A PARTY OF YACHT CLUB MEMBERS, PROB-ABLY MID-1930S.

---

5   *The Commerical Appeal* 6/8/1902
6   *ibid*

club's history is not how much it has changed, but its successful survival as a small community through the tumultuous changes of the 20th century. The census of 1900, the closest taken to the time of the MYC's founding, listed the population of Memphis as 102,320.[7] The city was home to the largest mule market in the world, among other things, due to the crossroads provided by the river and the new railroads. Boating may have been common, but automobiles were still uncommon on the city streets. Most of the traffic was still horse-drawn, including city services like garbage collection and fire engines. And even garbage collection was a new service, having previously been performed by herds of pigs.[8]

Boats had a different relevance on the river in the early twentieth century. There was no automobile traffic across the Mississippi at Memphis until the Harahan Bridge was finished in 1917. Principally a locomotive bridge, its outer trusses were "paved" with wooden planks to allow cars to pass in a single file. When the bridge burned in 1928, Memphis and Arkansas were again disconnected. Seeing an opportunity, Memphis businessmen Russell Warner and Herman Tambell pooled their resources of a large boat and a barge to ferry cars across the river.

---

7   Charles Wann Crawford, *Yesterday's Memphis*. (E.A. Seemann Publishing, Inc. Miami, 1976) 71
8   Crawford, 72-73

Raging River

Several members of the Memphis Yacht Club played important roles –heroic roles- during the terrible flooding of early 1937. Over the course of the 20th century there were several major floods along the Mississippi. Although the levee system has continually improved to prevent or mitigate flooding, from time to time the raw power of the continent's largest river simply overwhelms our defenses. In 1937, the river rose to a level of 48.7 feet, causing some 60,000 displaced persons to seek refuge in Memphis.[9]

Club member Henry Ellis remembers the flood from his childhood, recalling the surprise of Memphians at the sudden rise of the river. Having gone downtown to get a haircut, the men in the barbershop did not believe him when he told them that the water had risen over the railroad tracks at the foot of Beale Street. He wagered the

9   Bartholomew Sullivan. "Deluge of '37 compounded ruin of the Depression," in *The Commercial Appeal,* 4/16/1997.

change in his pocket that it was so, and promptly collected from the bewildered barber when a newspaper corroborating his story was dropped at the door of the shop.

The actions of a number of local men, some of whom were yacht club members, was commemorated in the February 18, 1937 edition of the Memphis Press-Scimitar under the headline, "Heroes of the Flood: Beyond the Call of Duty, They Worked in Water and Cold Without Rest or Food; Thinking First of Those in Distress." Chief among them was Dr. Louis Leroy, one of the Memphis Yacht Club's most illustrious members. During the flood he was the director of the American Red Cross rescue division from Cairo, IL to Rosedale, MS. He was responsible for "organizing the largest fleet of boats ever assembled on fresh water, [and] spending five tense days and several sleepless nights coordinating 1000 of these rescue boats into mosquito fleets." It was his "tireless drive that kept men heading 'johnboats' into sloughs and dense woods in order to save lives."

Also celebrated was long-time member Ollie W. McClure, an automobile salesman who rescued women and children stranded on an island north of Memphis. He also used his boat to take provisions

PAGE RIGHT: CLUB BOATERS MAN A NET DURING A DAY TRIP DOWN THE RIVER.

COURTESY OF BOB SCHWARTZ.

to stranded farmers. The newspaper also commended Reverend Alfred Loaring-Clark, Francis Gee, Tommie Franks, George Butler, John Fabrick Jr., Ceylon Frazer, Eddie Holman, Raymond Skinner, Clarice Lawrence, D. T. Perkins, and Jimmie Roberts. The article concluded that "it was these men who formed the backbone of refugee work." Their knowledge of the river, centralized location and equipment, and sense of civic duty made the heroics of yacht club members possible during the winter of 1937.

In addition to their contributions to flood relief efforts, there is considerably more to say about Dr. Leroy and O. W. McClure, whose connections to the club and the river spanned decades. McClure was born in 1895 and joined the club in the 1920's. After working as an auto salesman, he moved with his family to Corinth, MS, where he ran a Chris Craft dealership. He was not only a member, but sold and serviced boats on the river. An experienced boater, he taught others how to safely operate boats on the river, as when he bought a boat for his 15-year-old daughter, Mary Margaret (Buck).

Dr. Leroy's leadership during the '37 floods was perhaps his most beneficent claim to fame, but it was not his only one; not even his most noted one. Originally from Massachusetts, he moved to Tennessee in 1899 to take a post as professor of pathology and bacteriology at Vanderbilt University. During that time he was the state expert on smallpox. His obituary noted the following: "He was a man of indomitable spirit, whose energy carried him into many diversified fields. He was noted as a medical expert in legal proceedings. He drove the first automobile in Tennessee…He installed the first X-ray in Tennessee…Always interested in politics and world events, he frequently expressed opinions on various issues. Long before Pearl Harbor he was urging repeal of the neutrality act, saying, 'The Germans will take care of slaves just as sportsmen care for quail –until the hunting season.'" He was also a member of the American Board of Internal Medicine. He served as a volunteer for the Coast Guard Temporary Reserve at the outbreak of WWII. He authored several books, and as "an outstanding chess player, he once played Emanuel Lasker, then world's champion, to a draw."[1]

As if all of that were not enough to fill a life, it omits his most notorious achievement. He worked and planned for years to best the record time for sailing up the Mississippi from New Orleans to St. Louis. That record was set in 1870, when the *Robert E. Lee* arrived at the St. Louis wharf 90 hours and 14 minutes after leaving New Orleans.[2] He began planning the voyage in 1913, and

PAGE RIGHT: THE RIVER AT DUSK.

FOLLOWING PAGE: THE MEMPHIS YACHT CLUB CLUBHOUSE, COMPLETED IN 1948.

COURTESY OF BOB SCHWARTZ

1   *Memphis Press Schmitar* 5/10/1944
2   Paul R. Coppock, *Memphis Sketches*. (Friends of Memphis and Shelby County Libraries, 1976) 7.

MYC

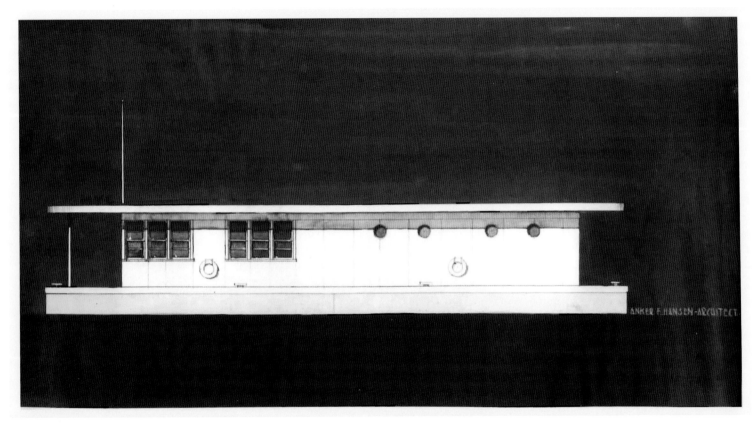

made three unsuccessful attempts starting in 1927. Although his first attempts were plagued by motor trouble and errant driftwood, he remained undeterred. He imported special mahogany, which he used to build the hull of the Bogie in his back yard.[3] In that boat, powered by a 150-horsepower motor, Dr. Leroy went on to set a new record: "On July 21, 1929, the Bogie left New Orleans in a race for 'five cents in cash and a million dollars in honor' against George M. Cox of New Orleans in the Martha Jane…Telegraph services flashed news of his progress, and comparisons with time made by the Robert E. Lee for the same distances, throughout the nation."[4] The Bogie cruised into St. Louis 87 hours and 31 minutes after leaving the Crescent City, shattering a record that had stood for nearly sixty years. The Bogie later burned, but Leroy went on to have several boats, all with supernatural names: the Djinn, and Pan.

By the 1940s, the Memphis Yacht Club membership was already middle-aged, with seasoned boaters who frequently travelled with their families together in flotillas. Around that time the old boathouse was replaced. Architect Anker F. Hansen designed a new single-story floating boathouse to go at the foot of Poplar Avenue. The long-time manager of the club during these years was Ray Crosier, a man famous for his hospitality. The yacht

3   *Memphis Press Schmitar* 5/10/1944
4   *The Commercial Appeal* 5/10/1944

PREVIOUS PAGE: A VIEW OF THE WATERFRONT, INCLUDING MUD ISLAND PRIOR TO DEVELOPMENT.

COURTESY OF THE MEMPHIS AND SHELBY COUNTY ROOM, MEMPHIS PUBLIC LIBRARY & INFORMATION CENTER

PAGE LEFT: ARCHITECT ANKER HANSEN'S DRAWING FOR THE NEW MYC CLUBHOUSE OF 1948.

MARCH 14, 1947:
THIS FLOATING DRY
DOCK, BUILT BY
MR. HAWKINS AND
DESIGNED BY MR.
ANKER HANSEN
WAS PUT IN THE
WOLF RIVER BY
SOUTHERN TRANS-
FER CO.'S CRAIN.
MR. HAWKINS
CLIMBS ABOARD
TO DIRECT PLACE-
MENT.

CLAYTON KREGER IS MOVING HIS CRUISER TO AVOID ANY CONTACT BETWEEN THE DRY DOCK AND HIS BOAT. THE DRY DOCK WEIGHED APPROXIMATELY TWO TONS AND CAN PROBABLY LIFT EIGHT.

club played host not just to its members, but to a diverse array of travelers on the river –a tradition that continues to the present day. People travelling by canoe would frequently stay overnight in the boathouse. Boats of all sizes travelling up and down river would stop for food, fuel, repairs, and advice. Among the documents from early days of the yacht club are letters from passersby thanking Crosier and others for their help and hospitality. Then as now, the Memphis Yacht Club offered one of the few oases for travelers from St. Louis to the Gulf.

On at least one occasion, Crosier talked to the newspaper about the lively nature of the yacht club's environs. An interview with him ran under the headline, "River Is a Strong Lure: Some Queer Goings-On." Crosier had seen a well-dressed woman step off the stone bank into the deep mud of the Wolf River waterfront: "She waded in neck deep with all of her clothes on and with her purse still hung from a strap about her neck…She took hold of one of the spars that run out to the Yacht Club. I don't know what she was trying to do. I told her to go back where she came from. She turned around and walked back up the hill. She was covered in mud. She lost her shoes in the mud. I called the police." The following day he witnessed another odd spectacle when a man took off his trousers, waded into the river, filled a bucket with water, took it ashore and drank it. "Somebody else called the police," Mr. Crosier said. "Two

PAGE RIGHT: HOMEWARD BOUND, BUDDY MCKNIGHT HAS PLACED THE DRY DOCK IN TOW AND HEADS FOR THE YACHT CLUB.

48

ambulances came. They took him away." In another incident, two high school girls were playing in the mud with their shoes off. One of them cut her foot on some glass, and Crosier let them use the Yacht Club facilities to wash off her cut.

PREVIOUS PAGE LEFT: A VIEW OF THE CLUBHOUSE FROM THE WATER.

PREVIOUS PAGE RIGHT: BILL NOLAN, CENTER, PAINTING THE HULL OF A COAST GUARD BOAT.

COURTESY OF BOB SCHWARTZ.

PAGE LEFT: THE CLUBHOUSE AND BOATHOUSES.

FOLLOWING SPREAD: TWO VIEWS OF A FAMILY LIVING IN A TENT ON MIDDLE BAR. THE ISLANDS OF THE MISSISSIPPI WERE HOME TO MANY SUCH PEOPLE, SOME OF WHOM TRADED WITH VISITING YACHT CLUB BOATERS.

COURTESY OF BOB SCHWARTZ.

At the new boathouse, member Bob Jorgensen built a gangway to connect the floating barge to the shore. He also constructed large anchors to hold the clubhouse in place. Every once in a while, a large storm would come through and push the clubhouse and attached boathouses up onto the cobblestones. They used the anchors to wench the floating structures back out onto the water. In the late 40s they also constructed a floating dry dock for the club. Until then, the only dry dock was operated by Howard Ainsley on a floating barge in the river. Ainsley went on to operate one of the first pleasure cruise boats out of Memphis, which he fashioned out of a WWII landing craft.

Its new location at the foot of Poplar brought the Memphis Yacht Club into closer contact with Mud Island and some new neighbors. For a long time Mud Island remained an unincorporated, unofficial part of Memphis inhabited by poor squatters. Long before their move to Mud Island, club members were well acquainted with the people and culture of life on Mississippi's islands. It is interesting

to note that Mud Island as we know it is almost as old as the Yacht Club: "Mud Island was formed by an eddy in 1910 which deposited mud and gravel against the stern of the gunboat Aphrodite,...a Federal gunboat which had been used in the Spanish American War."[1] The gunboat had travelled up river with a full naval crew, destined for the Missouri State Naval Reserves. But finding the river too shallow at Memphis, it had to be abandoned for three years. When the tide rose and the Aphrodite finally left, a small sandbar had formed at the foot of Court St. Years of river deposits built up the sandbar known today as Mud Island.

Mud Island and the Hen and Chicken islands were frequent destinations for yacht club boaters. Back in the 40s the islands were still populated by small groups of people: families, squatters, and hermits farmed and fished for a living. Yacht club member Bob Schwartz recalls the days from his childhood spent on the islands playing and meeting locals. Together with his Boy Scout troop he built a small log cabin on one of the islands. When the rising river swept away all but the roof of the cabin, they gave it to the island's resident hermit, Adolph Ueltschi. Known to yacht club boaters as "Old Man of the Island," "The Hermit of Middle Bar," or simply as Adolph, he lived a pioneer lifestyle

1   Joe Curtis, "The Beginning of Mud Island," in *A Great Island Called Mud*, Compiled by William F. Currotto. (Patchwork Books, 1993)

PAGE RIGHT: THE SCHWARTZ CHILDREN BUILDING A LOG CABIN ON MIDDLE BAR ISLAND IN THE 1940'S.

FOLLOWING SPREAD: TWO VIEWS OF THE COMPLETED CABIN.

COURTESY OF BOB SCHWARTZ.

and only travelled to the mainland in his skiff to sell the fish he caught.

Although he made do with very basic essentials, he was known as a highly inventive man who crafted things with great ingenuity. He built a two-room house on Middle Bar out of corrugated tin, painting it dark brown. To keep out the north wind during the winter months, he put up a wooden wall on the north side of the cabin. "Even his stovewood was cut in exact lengths, stacked in exact piles. His fireplace, kitchen stove, pots and pans and floor indicated a love of cleanliness and orderliness."[2] He made many of his own tools, brooms, and farming implements, with which he farmed several acres. He raised chickens on a homemade feed of ground fish heads, which Bob Schwartz suspected was the reason they laid eggs with shells so hard "you'd have to crack them open on a rock." To keep track of time, he fashioned a wooden calendar and moved a little peg from day to day.

Although he hailed originally from Germany, no one ever knew exactly where he came from, or for that matter, exactly where he went. Among other things, Adolph grew corn, peanuts, and flowers which he would trade with visiting yacht club

---

2 *The Commercial Appeal*, 2/7/1946

boaters. During their final visit with the hermit, Schwartz and his father gathered that he could use a bellows for smelting iron. They returned some time later, lugging the heavy equipment across the island only to find the cabin ransacked and Adolph missing. The front door, with homemade locks described as "ingenious," had been kicked open. Among the disheveled belongings, they found his rifle, which had been misfired. His calendar was pegged January 26, 1946. His skiff was missing and he was never seen or heard from again.[3]

Having lived on the margin of society and leaving no corpse, there was little in the manner of a police investigation. But Bob Schwartz pieced together the probable fate of the hermit. A couple of weeks after his disappearance, a man named Boges found Adolph's abandoned skiff tied up on the bank near the mouth of the Loosahatchie. However, the river had risen so much since his vanishing that the skiff would have been tied much lower down the bank. Boges claimed that he had found the skiff tied in its present position just after Adolph went missing, so it was clear that he was lying. Furthermore, Boges' own cousin suggested he had killed him. And that was that.

---

3   *The Commercial Appeal*, 2/7/1946

Most of the mentions of the Memphis Yacht Club in the papers of the 1940s revolved around the comings and goings of "snowbirds," yacht owners from the North passing through Memphis to escape for the winter. An article from the Commercial Appeal dated November 11, 1948 quoted manager J. W. Crosier as saying yachts were passing through Memphis at a rate of about one a day.

PAGE LEFT: MEMPHIS BOATERS SPENDING THE DAY ON A SANDBAR.

RIGHT: YOUNG YACHT CLUBBERS SPRINTING UP A SANDBANK.

PHOTOS COURTESY OF BOB SCHWARTZ

MYC

They would come from as far away as Long Island, NY, sailing up the Hudson, through the Great Lakes to Chicago, and down the Illinois and Mississippi. Travelers coming up and down the Mississippi would be greeted first by the sight of a clubhouse floating alongside some forty private boathouses and slips, all tied together. Inside the clubhouse lived a talking Myna bird. His vocabulary was restricted to squawking "Memphis Yacht!" whenever the phone rang.

Memphians were no strangers to long voyages, but most of the club's activities then as now consisted mainly of local pleasure boating. Little islands with beaches like Middle Bar always made for nice, quick getaways. A sandy beach provided the perfect place to park a boat and spend the day. Picnics and fish fries with friends and family, and finding time to relax away from the city have always been at the core of the club.

When the country geared up for war in 1941, members of the Memphis Yacht Club were ready to do their part. Members who were too senior to serve in the regular armed forces joined the Coast Guard Auxiliary Reserve. Together with the Coast Guard they helped patrol the Mississippi, watching for suspicious cargo or a German U-Boat. While no evidence exists to suggest a German submarine ever travelled up the Mississippi,

PAGE LEFT: MEMBERS OF THE COAST GUARD PRACTICE STORMING A BEACH NEAR MEMPHIS DURING WWII. YACHT CLUB MEMBERS WERE ACTIVELY INVOLVED WITH THE COAST GUARD, MANY SERVING IN THE COAST GUARD AUXILIARY RESERVE.

COURTESY OF BOB SCHWARTZ.

LEFT AND RIGHT: 1940'S.
MEMPHIS BOATERS, POLICE,
AND THE COAST GUARD
SURVEY THE DAMAGE FROM AN
AMERICAN AIRLINES DC3 THAT
CRASHED IN THE RIVER NEAR
COW ISLAND.

COURTESY OF BOB SCHWARTZ.

MYC

nearly sixty vessels were sunk by torpedoes in the Gulf of Mexico during the first two years of the war, including a tanker at the mouth of the river.

Boating on the Mississippi has never been without its perils. The river can be unforgiving even to seasoned boaters. In times of danger, the shore can be like a mirage as inaccessible as for a boat lost at sea. The rapid current, hidden submerged banks, and barge traffic are just a few of the river's crucibles. An article from June 20, 1948 illuminates one of the dangers faced by a yacht club family. Mr. and Mrs. William M. Bell were boating with their children on the Tennessee River near Guntersville, Alabama, when their vessel, the *Belle of Memphis,* caught fire and burned on the water. "Mr. Bell suffered second degree burns while his wife and their four passengers narrowly escaped injury or death."[1]

Time and again, members of the Memphis Yacht Club have come to the aid of people in danger. Norman Blackley recalls saving men from a plane that crashed in the river. He was cruising up river when a small airplane came down swiftly, nearly hitting his boat before crashing into the water: "It immediately

---

1   *The Commercial Appeal*, 6/20/1948

ABOVE: FROM LEFT, HELEN GEORGI, BILL BECK, NORMAN BLACKLEY, AND CHARLES COOK.

LEFT: HAM SMYTHE.

MYC

sank, and two people swam out of the plane. I put my ladder down and they climbed up on my boat."

Henry Ellis, who runs the William C. Ellis & Sons Iron Works on Front St., has a couple of stories about helping out stranded boaters on the river. Once he was headed down the river when he came upon a tugboat stranded at Star Landing. He took their mechanic on board and headed back to Memphis for repair equipment. On their way back to the city in the dead of night, a powerful storm came over the river. They continued through the storm toward the city, only to pass the stranded tug they had been helping earlier. Ellis says that was when he decided to buy a compass. On another occasion, he was headed up the river with his friend Russell Warner. They passed a fifty-foot vessel and three smaller ones. Ellis was steering the boat through driftwood when Warner noticed that the wake of the big boat had swamped the several smaller ones. They turned around and fished the men out the river, one of whom was still trying to save his sinking boat. Ellis and Warner helped them salvage what they could of the boats and saw them safely to the shore. As it turned out, the three men saved were prominent attorneys in Memphis, and were quite embarrassed at their predicament. Ellis received a letter of thanks from them the following day with

the addendum that they were thankful their names were known only to him.

Running a family business that's been around since 1862, Ellis grew up next to the river and spent a lot of time in the yacht club. In addition to keeping his own boat, his firm at one time operated five tugboats. In the 1970s, he participated in a series of tugboat races known as The Great Mississippi River Race. In an early effort to draw Memphians' attention back downtown and to the river, he and several friends raced their tugboats on a course that ran up and down the river between the old and new bridges. During one of the races, one of the participants showed up pushing a long barge. He tried to use the barge as an advantage when making the first turn, cutting off the others. Despite the extra "nose" attached to the tug, Ellis passed him on the way back downstream in the Ira Vaughn, and won the race.

Elbie Smith took over as manager of the Yacht Club from Ray Crosier sometime in the early 1950s. A former shoe salesman, he also possessed a great knack for salvaging and repairing boats. Together with Lewis Richards, he oversaw operations and maintained the club during the 1950s and 60s. At one point Smith acquired an historic boat from the Army Corps of Engineers, the Plover. Designed

PAGE LEFT: MEMBERS OF THE COAST GUARD RESERVE AND THE YACHT CLUB.

RIGHT: A FISHERMAN SHOWS HIS CATCH.

PHOTOS COURTESY OF BOB SCHWARTZ.

MYC

to escort senators, dignitaries, and engineers to observe the building of the levees, it had one of the largest engines of any boat of its kind. As an escort boat, it had to accommodate many people and move quickly from place to place. As such, it was thirty feet long and built to do 50mph on the river. Smith modified the boat by taking the cabin off the front and moving it to the rear, as a little dog house over two bunks.

BOTTOM LEFT: THE BROWN FAMILY IN THEIR BOAT

BOTTOM RIGHT: FROM LEFT, BOB SCHWARTZ, DANNY WOOD, BOB JORGENSEN, AND ROY SMITH.

PAGE RIGHT: A BOAT SINKS AFTER ITS HULL IS CRUSHED BY THE ICE BLANKETING THE MISSISSIPPI IN THE WINTER OF 1939.

COURTESY OF BOB SCHWARTZ.

PAGE LEFT: THE ZORILLA BROTHERS HOLD UP TWO GIGANTIC CATFISH.

ABOVE: A PORTRAIT OF THE MAN WHO KEPT THE MISSISSIPPI RIVER LIT AT NIGHT, TRAVELLING UP AND DOWN THE RIVER TO REFILL THE KEROSENE LAMPS USED FOR NAVIGATION.

RIGHT: JAY CROZIER, LONG TIME MANAGER OF THE YACHT CLUB. MEMBERS RECALL THAT HE WORE A SUIT EVERY DAY.

PHOTOS COURTESY OF BOB SCHWARTZ

MYC

NO WAKE AREA

A New Era

When construction began on Mud Island, the Yacht Club had to move. It was in 1977 that plans were drawn up to give up the old clubhouse and build a new one. It was a sad occasion for many members who had grown up with the club in its location at the foot of Poplar Avenue. Many had to say good-bye to old boathouses, each of which had gained its own unique character over the years. A cozy new headquarters was established just a stone's throw away on Mud Island. The old dry dock managed to escape demolition, ferried across the channel to the new location. This is the marina as we know it today.

The old boathouses may be gone, but the traditions of the Memphis Yacht Club continue to thrive. The Southern hospitality that animated the life of the club in earlier days is alive and well. The Yacht Club still provides an invaluable service to boaters from out of town as an oasis on the Mississippi. Along with larger vessels, it has become a port-of-call for kayakers. Not long ago two men in kayaks stopped off at the club on a journey that began in Montana. This seems especially fitting since the club originally grew from small canoeing clubs.

Today the Memphis Yacht Club serves its members as well as the larger community. Its members promote responsibility on the river in boating safety and environmentalism. Committed to the greening of the Memphis harbor, they raised over $30,000 for a sanitation boat to pump waste out of the harbor. The club has also invested in oil booms that help prevent contamination of the river. On January 11, 2011 they helped the Coast Guard by spreading their oil booms around a sinking boat. That is the kind of preparedness that characterizes the club's environmental awareness. Green flags fly on their boats as symbols of this commitment.

In addition to teaching about boating safety, the Yacht Club works actively to ensure the safety of river-goers. They supervise river activities such as the annual Green Canoe Race. They also monitor emergency radio channels, ready to assist boaters in need on the Mississippi.

More broadly, the Memphis Yacht Club maintains a culture and way of life that have in many ways disappeared. The club arose in a time when Memphis was much more connected to the river, with the cultural life of the city confined to a much smaller area near its banks. The furious activity that once animated the Memphis harbor has gently subsided. What was once the lumber and mule-trading capital of the world has become one of the world's largest centers for shipping by air.

Today it can be easy to forget that the river is there, and the popular consciousness is full of misunderstandings about the Mississippi. It is far more than a highway of barge traffic, and the Yacht Club provides people with a connection to that knowledge. For members, the river is a playground, a vast and largely untamed natural wilderness. To spend a day on one of the river's many islands is to experience what the country was like long before it was inhabited. Together, the members of the Yacht Club have developed the kind of working knowledge of the river that is dearly bought –only with time, care, and experience.

83

Recollections

My Trip on the *Interlude*

By Roy Hendrix

April, 2002

I have recently completed a paper recounting my many trips over the last 27 or so years on my boats, as well as (and more frequently) on the boats of my friends. In that paper I mentioned briefly a trip I took in the Interlude, a sailboat owned by my friend, Elbie Smith. I have already told my local boating friends about this almost disastrous trip. Several of them have said I should reduce my recollections to writing. I said that this trip should be the subject of its own paper. Well, here are the gruesome details of said trip.

Elbie Smith was a truly unique individual. He was the long-time manager of the Memphis Yacht Club and that is where I first met him back in the 70's when I first started boating in a serious way. Back then, and for many years until the opening of the Tenn-Tom Waterway, the only way for downstream-bound boats to get to the open Gulf, and world-wide points from there, was to pass Memphis and the Memphis Yacht Club en-route. In this process, many boaters would only get this far on their "journey of a lifetime." They would then, for various reasons, cool on the venture. Some would leave the boat here, intending to return and resume their journey, and then would call the Yacht Club and tell the manager they wished to sell their boat. Others would simply get this far, decide that the

whole idea of such a trip was a bad mistake and try to sell the boat before returning home, in some cases almost giving it away. By one of these routes, Elbie, being Club Manager and the one to first find out about the potential bargain sale, became the owner (for a song) of a forty-two foot wooden sailboat, the Interlude.

Over the intervening years, Elbie reworked the boat (or so we thought), scavenging instruments, equipment, electronics, even replacing the little "atomic four" auxiliary engine with a small diesel he somehow acquired. Being long-time divorced, and with only one child, a daughter who lived in or near Boston, his aim was to eventually take the boat and visit her. This would involve taking the Interlude down the Mississippi to New Orleans, then across the Gulf of Mexico, around through the Keys, up the East Coast, ultimately arriving at Boston, or more accurately, Martha's Vineyard, where his daughter and her husband had a summer home.

As the years went by, Elbie began telling all us boating friends that the time was about ripe for the trip to begin. I had really not paid much attention to the Interlude, other than to know that he had been "working on the boat and preparing for the trip" for years. He set a tentative departure date from Memphis, and began assembling crews to assist him in making the voyage. He was only able to assemble crews for the first two legs: (1) Memphis to New Orleans, the crew being two of his oldest and most experienced boating friends, Alfred Anderson and Bob Jorgensen; and (2) New Orleans across the Gulf, crossing the Keys at Marathon, Fla., and on up to Miami, the crew being yours truly, Tommy Hunt, and Richard Walker. We were all experienced boaters, and Richard was also an experienced sailor. His experience just about saved the day, as will be explained later.

The appointed day came, and I was with a sizeable group of friends who witnessed their departure from the Mud Island Marina docks. This is where the old Memphis Yacht Club had moved from its

RIGHT: MARGERIE SCHWARTZ CONSTRUCTING ONE OF HER MANY WATERCOLORS. WITH SO MUCH TIME SPENT ON THE RIVER, HER PAINTINGS FREQUENTLY FEATURED NAUTICAL THEMES.

BELOW, A COAST GUARD BOAT.

FOLLOWING PAGE: BOYS FROM THE SEA SCOUTS HEADED DOWN RIVER IN THEIR BOAT, A RUM RUNNER SEIZED BY THE COAST GUARD IN THE GULF.

COURTESY OF BOB SCHWARTZ.

MYC

location on the cobblestones when Mud Island Park and Marina opened in 1982. I am not really sure when this voyage began, but I do know that it was after 1982, when Mud Island Marina opened. There was much excitement and fanfare, as many of us wished them well on this, the beginning of a very long voyage. I did notice that Bob and Alfred were throwing all sorts of junk off the boat over Elbie's objections, continuing to do so until the very moment they cast off and got underway. This would prove to be an omen of what lay ahead for us on the later leg of the trip.

Richard, Tommy and I were to fly down and meet them at Shubert's Marina on Lake Pontchartrain at New Orleans. We did so and were waiting for them at the Marina when they arrived. We thought it strange when Alfred and Bob, our good friends for many years, jumped off the Interlude as if somebody had a loaded .45 at their heads and they really feared they would be shot. They hardly even spoke. We later learned that they had a nearly disastrous trip on the 650-mile down-river trip, during which they were under power, not sail. The term "under power" should be used very loosely, as that was one of their major problems. We learned that the auxiliary diesel gave constant problems, died at very crucial times, and on more than a few occasions left them drifting without power into the path of a huge tow of barges. This could have had fatal results. Only restarting the engine at the last minute saved them. We were later to learn of this engine problem on our voyage across the Gulf.

This was on a Saturday and we spent the rest of the day shopping for provisions for our leg of the trip, which was to be largely under sail over the open Gulf. We even went down to the French Quarter for dinner, had a great time and spent a good night aboard the Interlude docked at the Marina. Tommy and I had the "V" berths forward, and Elbie and Richard had the two single berths amid-ship. The next day, Sunday, we motored out through Lake Pontchartrain, intending to exit at the extreme east end and go through a point

LEFT: COLONEL ROANE WAR-
ING, CLUB MEMBER WHO
COMMANDED THE 2ND TEN-
NESSEE INFANTRY DIVISION IN
WWI. HE RAN THE MEMPHIS
STREETCAR COMPANY AND WAS
ACTIVE IN ORGANIZING VET-
ERANS' GROUPS THAT BECAME
THE AMERICAN LEGION.

LEFT: A MAN IN A DIVING SUIT
COMES OUT OF THE RIVER
AFTER WORKING TO BUOY THE
CLUBHOUSE, WHICH PARTIALLY
SANK IN 1940.

COURTESY OF BOB SCHWARTZ.

MYC

called "The Narrows," then on out into the Gulf. We did not question this decision by Elbie, our Captain. We later had to rather forcefully question some of his decisions. Having boated in this area previously, I would have exited through the Inter-coastal Waterway and much more easily found the open water. The route he chose involved many delays in going through highway draw-bridges. It took most of the day, but we did have a slow and rather enjoyable time.

By the time we cleared The Narrows into the Gulf, it was early evening and Elbie decided we should anchor out for the night, which we did, having a pleasant evening and night in the calm shelter of an island. This was to be the last of such pleasurable nights for the balance of the trip, which ended the following Sunday. The next morning we set sail on our course for Marathon, about 135 degrees as I recall. We soon learned of the boat's severe limitations. The first was that it was open cockpit with a tiller, not a wheel. This made steering very, very difficult under sail, with the boat heeling over se-verely and the helmsman being totally exposed to the open weather. It also made the compass, which was well forward behind the wind screen, very hard to see, even in the daylight, and extremely hard to see at night. This was our only means of navigation.

Further, the fact of only having a tiller was a nightmare and took constant and consider-able strength on the part of the helmsman on duty. We soon discovered that by rigging a line from a clete on the side of the cockpit, wrapping it around the tiller while holding the working end, then sitting crosswise in the cockpit and bracing one's legs on the lower side, was the only way the helmsman could handle the tiller and remain on course. This made long hours at the helm very dif-ficult.

The second main problem (or so we thought at the time) was that the jib sail was much too large, and caused us to heel over much more than would have been the case of the proper sized jib. The boom actually dipped into the water.

But the absolutely worst condition was that, being a wooden boat, and one which had not in many years been in open water, the planking had dried out and contracted above the water line. Once we got under sail, heeling over and moving in the water, the boat leaked like a sieve. The bow spray leaked into our forward bunks such as to make them totally uninhabitable. We could only sleep in the two middle single bunks, two at a time. It is hard to list all the problems, but others stand out. Elbie had scrounged a "radar reflector" (as he had scrounged all the other sails, equipment, electronics, etc.) which he hauled up to the top of the mast. This was supposed to make us a better target to other vessels, particularly the many shrimp boats which were all over the place. At night, the lights from these shrimp boats were visible from horizon to horizon. This reflector spun violently in the wind, like a buzz-saw, and quickly chewed up much of the tops of the sails, as well as the rigging.

We were then faced with taking the sails down and trying to repair them so they could be used. We also had to repair and redo the rigging. This problem took most of the first day, as we could not get underway with the sails down. We managed somehow to make the needed repairs. We had many other problems. The auxiliary diesel engine had constant cooling and exhaust problems. The bilge pumps and all intake strainers became clogged with sawdust, wood chips and other debris after running for only short periods, then would require being emptied and cleaned.

We were soon way out into the Gulf, and found that, due to the brisk wind being "on our nose" and due to our problems with the huge and incorrect jib, we could not tack closer than about 45 degrees to our course. No matter how we worked it, we just seemed to get farther and farther south and west of our course.

We divided the duty into two-man watches, four on and four off, Tommy and me, then Elbie and Richard. Our problems with the faulty engine, which we attempted to run from time to time to assist us in maintaining our course, continued until we finally wrote it off as inoperable unless in an absolute emergency, and very doubtful even then. The boat continued to leak very badly. One night in the middle of the Gulf when Tommy and I had the 8pm to midnight watch, at about 11:45 I decided to shine a flashlight down into the cabin to begin rousing them to come on watch and relieve us promptly at mid-night. We were dog tired and did not want them to be even one minute late. To my astonishment, I saw nothing but water in the cabin and their tennis shoes floating back and forth. The water was nearly up to their bunks and it seemed very clear that we were in grave danger of sinking. I yelled at them and they came splashing through the water to top-side. We quickly activated the electric bilge pump in the lazaret. While Elbie was getting it ready, the rest of us manned the manual bilge pumps.

ABOVE: BUDDY AND TOMMY MCKNIGHT MOTORING ACROSS THE HARBOR.

FOLLOWING PAGE: THE OLD FLOATING BOATHOUSES.

COURTESY OF BOB SCHWARTZ

We thought our prayers had been answered, but they were soon dashed. We discovered that the pump had a two-cycle engine, where the oil and gas had to be mixed. Of course, Elbie had not pre-mixed any oil and gas, so we had to do so under ten foot swells, with the boat badly heeling over and taking on water. We finally got the mixing done, fueled up the pump's engine and it started and came to life. We thought we were saved. But the pump would not start pumping and we saw that it needed to be primed.

I remember well sitting in the cockpit and dipping a galley cooking pan directly into the water, we were heeled over that far that I easily reached the water without getting my arm wet. After pouring several pans full of water directly into the outlet hose, we were delighted when it started spouting a huge stream of water overboard. We were crushed when after only a few minutes the intake hose line collapsed, it being a hose type which was not suited for the pickup side and could have only been used on the outflow side of any pump. It was similar type hose you might see on a dryer exhaust vent. Never would it stand up to being an intake hose under internal pressure. As no other usable hose was on board, we had to begin a round-the-clock regimen of manning the two manual bilge pumps. As I recall, each crew member would pump about 200 strokes and would then be relieved. The leaking finally subsided to some manageable extent when all the planking on the boat swelled. The manual pumping had to be continued periodically, nevertheless, throughout the rest of the voyage.

A most welcome dawn broke finally after that terrible night and it was beautiful. We continued several more days and nights of taking on a southerly course for eight or so hours, then revering to a northeasterly course for a similar period. Our inability to tack anywhere near the wind continued to be a pervasive problem. We really did not have any real idea of our position, though we suspected we were going ever further south and west, far off our course. Elbie had told us before we left Memphis that he had a Loran on board. Yes he did have one, but it was a very old, first generation Loran which took a rocket scientist to operate with any useable accuracy. It was nothing like the ones we were used to. It took all sorts of interpreting of many columns of meaningless signals, very much like some sort of oscilloscope, then consulting a book of tables, then plotting and plotting on your charts. It was of no use whatsoever.

While we were discussing our rapidly worsening situation, we heard a jet aircraft approaching from behind us and it was clearly the U.S. Coast Guard. They flew low and directly over us and I felt sure they were trying to contact us, as we were the only boat visible on the horizon. I ran below and got on Channel 16 on the miserable little VHF Marine radio Elbie had scrounged and called them. They immediately answered and asked our name, home port, destination, and "souls on board," which I promptly gave them. I started to tell them of our dire straits, but decided not to do so at that time.

I did, however, tell them a little lie that our Loran was "giving us trouble" and could they give us the coordinates of our present position, which they promptly did. Then in a flash, they flew away.

When I plotted our position, I found that we were about 250 miles west-south-west of Tampa and about 250 miles south of Panama City, Fla. If we continued on our present course, we were headed straight for the Yucatan Peninsula. It was unthinkable to continue and Tommy and Richard and I concluded that we should reverse course and head for Apalachicola, the only realistic destination we could make under the present sailing conditions. Elbie would not hear to the changes we suggested, maintaining that we should continue to try for Marathon. We in effect "mutinied" against him and he was devastated, and sulked for quite a while, but gradually accepted the fact that we had made the correct decision under the circumstances. As it was, we were running short of food, had exhausted our meager water supply, and only had the melt from our ice coolers to drink and cook with. Our diesel engine inoperable, we had not propulsion or generating capability. To continue would have been courting real disaster.

Thus, in the late afternoon on that Thursday, we reversed course and made for Apalachicola, which, after much plotting and chart work we estimated reaching by Saturday evening. Thankfully, the weather was perfect. But the southeasterly wind from about 135 degrees at about 25 knots never stopped, generating ten foot swells day and night, squarely against our starboard beam. Sure enough, in the late afternoon on Saturday, we sighted land at Cape San Blas point, just about twenty miles west of Apalachicola. With darkness fast approaching, we decided we had no choice but to anchor out for the night. With no cover at all, we were forced to anchor in water about fifteen feet deep, completely unprotected, and dead on into the swells. Thus began the most miserable night I had ever spent. I am sure the others felt the same. The boat rolled and pitched like a bucking bronco and all we could do was to just take it as best we could.

ABOVE: AN ARMY CORP OF ENGINEERS WORK BOAT.

COURTESY OF BOB SCHWARTZ

Dawn finally came, though we thought it never would. Then came a problem we had never anticipated, that being having to "sail" off an anchorage dead into the wind. This is where Richard Walker's skills saved the day. We finally got off anchor and underway early that Sunday morning. The last great task remaining was that we would have to sail eastward into the famous West Pass to Apalachicola Bay. If you check your charts, you will see all sorts of warnings, cautions, symbols of the protruding masts of sunken ships, etc. The masts of the sunken boats were clearly visible as we made our way close by them. All of these cautioned strongly against use of this West Pass unless you were extremely familiar with it.

We had no choice. This meant that we had to sail essentially east, through this narrow and dangerous pass until it intersected with the regular manmade cut in the barrier island. Then, after making a ninety degree left turn, we could proceed all the way in to the city dock. Using all of Richard's skills, with all the help we could muster, we finally made it and docked without power at the City Dock about 5pm, having been six nights at sea. When we got off that boat, we all felt great to be on dry land. The very first thing we did was to thank our lucky stars for our safe arrival. Next we had several "welcoming drinks," and showered with the cold water hose on the dock with just our shorts on.

Elbie was never able to get any others to crew with him on the remainder of his voyage. We later heard that he went on solo and finally made it to Miami. There, he became dejected, abandoned his plans, sold the Interlude, and flew back to Memphis. He died about ten years ago. It is ironic that he sold the Interlude under the same circumstances in which he acquired it –a long anticipated, but ultimately abandoned, "trip of a lifetime."

And there you have it, my voyage on the Interlude.

RIGHT: PADDLERS REACH THE MISSISSIPPI DURING THE ANNUAL CANOE RACE.

BELOW, WEBBER PARTEE STANDING ON HIS BOAT. BEHIND HIM IS DR. LEROY'S BOAT, THE *GOBBLE UN*.

COURTESY OF BOB SCHWARTZ

MYC

A Yacht Club Story

By Helen Georgi

My husband, Charles, and I moved to Memphis from St. Louis in 1957. We had been married the previous year, and Charles had owned boats and enjoyed boating for many years.

After moving to Memphis, Charles bought our 43-foot Gulf Star, Happy Days, and we joined the Memphis Yacht Club. We thoroughly enjoyed the weekends docked on a sand bar with our boating friends –plus our holiday trips to Helena, Arkansas.

One summer, accompanied by our teenage daughter, Lisa, we took our boat to Lake Michigan.

Charles and some of his boating buddies took the boat to Chicago where Lisa and I boarded. We first docked on the Wisconsin shoreline and visited family in Door County during cherry picking season. We then crossed Lake Michigan, visited Mackinaw Island, and visited more family in Michigan. Then we began our return trip to Memphis, stopping overnight in Traverse City, then on to Chicago. Here Charles was intrigued to see a beautiful 48-foot Trojan for sale which he could not resist, and purchased it after selling our Gulf Star.

This lead to many HAPPY years of boating -here in the Memphis area and all over the state of Florida, where we always maintained a second home.

Before Charles' death in 1999, we docked our boat at Pickwick to be closer to Memphis. After his death, I sold our boat to a commercial pilot who took the boat to Miami, where he used it as a lay-over home between flights.

As of now, I believe that I am the only female lifetime member of the Memphis Yacht Club, with MANY MANY happy memories.

RIGHT: A YOUNG MAN IN A CANOE RIGGED WITH A PARA-CHUTE SAIL.

COURTESY OF BOB SCHWARTZ

BELOW, THE FRONT DECK OF THE OLD CLUBHOUSE.

FOLLOWING SPREAD: AN EXPERIMENTAL AIRCRAFT AS OBSERVED BY CLUB MEMBERS.

COURTESY OF BOB SCHWARTZ

MYC

Delightful Deck Drinks

Mississippi Bubbly Water

MIX 1 DRINK

½ oz. (or more) bourbon whiskey

½ teaspoon sugar

 Dash bitters

4-6 oz. champagne (chilled)

In a highball glass, muddle whiskey, ice, sugar, and bitters. Top off with champagne.

If made with Tennessee whiskey, it's nearly as potent as Mississippi River water.

MYC

All-Hands-on-Deck Sangria

SERVES 25 (MORE OR LESS, DEPENDING ON THIRST)

4   (750-ml) bottles zinfandel

½   cup brandy

¼   cup Cointreau

1   quart orange juice

½   cup lemon juice

¼   cup superfine sugar

12   ice cubes

1   quart club soda, chilled

3   oranges, thinly sliced

3   lemons, thinly sliced

Thoroughly chill all ingredients.

Pour wine, brandy and Cointreau into a large container.

In a separate container, stir orange and lemon juice with the sugar until sugar is thoroughly dissolved. Combine mixtures and stir to blend.

To keep the Sangria fresh, add ice cubes and soda to individual serving glasses and garnish with fruit slices and festive straws.

sandbar Smoothies

6 Drinks

1 large can frozen orange juice concentrate, undiluted

1 juice can gin or vodka

1 juice can half-and-half

1 juice can crushed ice

Pour undiluted juice into a blender. Add gin, half-and-half and ice; process until very smooth. Serve in champagne flutes.

Sick Bay Rum Remedy

PROPORTION TO SERVE ALL AFFLICTED CREW MEMBERS

1   part cream of coconut

1   part orange juice

4   parts pineapple juice

    Dark rum to taste

Combine cream of coconut and juices. Add rum and mix. Refrigerate until ready to serve.

Pour over ice and garnish with fruit kabobs made of chunks of pineapple, cherries and orange wedges.

The amount of rum used depends on just how much "medication" the crew needs.

Galley-Brewed Irish Cream

MAKES 6 CUPS

1   (14-oz.) can sweetened condensed milk

1½   cups heavy cream

¾   cup egg substitute

1   cup Irish whiskey

¼   teaspoon coconut extract

1½ tablespoons chocolate syrup

Process all ingredients in a blender for 30 seconds or until smooth. Pour into a clean glass jar or bottle and cover with a lid. Chill mixture for several weeks before using.

Serve chilled mixture in small glasses.

Not Jes Jivin' Java

MAKES 1 DRINK (OR 10; THE PROPORTIONS ARE THE SAME)

1   oz. coffee liqueur

1   oz. brandy

1   oz. half-and-half

Stir coffee liqueur and brandy over ice until well chilled. Pour into chilled glass.

Whip half-and-half til foamy. Spoon onto top of brandy/liqueur mix. Garnish with bits of coffee bean.

If you take your coffee with sugar, you may want to whisk some into the half-and-half.

115

Mud Island Sweet-TeaQuila

SERVES 6… WITH QUITE A WALLOP!

½   cup sugar

½   cup water

3   tablespoons fresh lemon juice

1   cup guava nectar

2   cups brewed tea

¾   cup silver tequila

   Lemon wedges for garnish

In a small saucepan, combine sugar and water. Stir mixture as it comes to a boil over medium-high heat. Continue to stir until sugar is dissolved.

Let cool to room temperature. Stir in lemon juice. In a pitcher combine lemon syrup, guava nectar, tea and tequila. Serve in tall glasses over ice. Garnish with a lemon wedge.

Wolf River Atomic Lemonade

MAKES 20 SERVINGS

1   cup sugar

1   cup water

½   cup mint leaves

½   teaspoon river water (optional)

5   cups club soda

4   cups vodka

4   cups fresh lemon juice

⅔   superfine sugar

    Lemon rounds and mint sprigs for garnish

To make simple syrup, heat sugar and water over low heat, stirring with a wooden spoon until sugar dissolves. Stop stirring and increase to medium heat. Simmer 2 minutes. Remove from heat and cool. Refrigerate at least 2 hours before using.

When ready to make lemonade, in a large bowl, mash mint leaves with simple syrup. Stir in club soda, vodka, lemon juice and sugar. Refrigerate. Pour into pitchers with lemon rounds and mint sprigs.

Need a little extra cash? An adults only lemonade stand serving this up on a hot afternoon would surely rake in the big bucks. It must be the river water that puts it over the top.

Tropical Moonshine

MAKES MORE THAN THE LAW ALLOWS

Fresh pineapples

Vodka

Large mason jar

Select very fresh pineapples, remove peel and cut into chunks. Pack pineapple chunks into the jar, filling to the edges and rim with pieces.

Pour in as much vodka as the jar will hold. Cover and let stand 5 to 6 days.

Refrigerate the jar for 6 to 12 hours before serving and pour directly from the tap into martini glasses. Use some of the pineapple for garnish.

This drink gives a whole new meaning to "punch" and it is certainly not your old granddaddy's moonshine! This concoction is easiest served from one of those big jars with a tap at bottom often sold as Sun Tea jars (sometimes found on eBay).

Dog Track Juleps

SERVES 8 TO 10

3 cups water

2-3 cups fresh spearmint leaves, lightly packed

2 cups sugar

1 cup bourbon

   sprigs of fresh mint

To make syrup, combine water, spearmint and sugar in a heavy saucepan. Bring to a boil over medium heat, stirring constantly until sugar dissolves. Boil gently for 3 minutes. Remove from heat, cover and chill at least 3 hours.

When ready to serve, strain syrup into a bowl or wide-mouth pitcher, pressing mint leaves to extract flavors. Discard mint.

For individual drinks, fill glasses or julep cups with finely crushed ice. Add 1 to 1½ jiggers of syrup and 1 to 1½ jiggers bourbon to each glass. Stir gently and garnish with fresh mint before serving.

Grinnin' Cabin Boys

FILLS 4 MARTINI GLASSES OR 2 TALL GLASSES

½   cup grapefruit juice

½   cup guava nectar

1½ ozs. fresh lemon juice

1   tablespoon superfine sugar

½   cup club soda

4   ozs. gold tequila

2   ozs. lemon liqueur

    Lemon slice for garnish

Combine grapefruit juice, guava juice, lemon juice, sugar, club soda, tequila and lemon liqueur in a blender.

For a frozen version, blend ingredients adding 10 to 12 ice cubes. For a non-frozen drink, blend ingredients together and pour over ice in a tall glass.

Garnish with lemon slice.

In this recipe, as with most other drink recipes requiring it, confectioner's sugar may be substituted for superfine.

Brass Monkeys

24 SERVINGS

1   *quart cranberry juice*

1   *large (10-oz.) can frozen orange juice concentrate*

3   *orange juice cans of water*

2   *quarts vodka*

Mix cranberry juice, frozen orange juice, water and vodka together and freeze in a gallon-size water jug. Remove from freezer a short while before serving, allowing it to defrost slightly.

Garnish with cinnamon sticks.

Alternatively, instead of allowing this mixture to thaw, use a fork to shave the ice concoction into small serving cups.

Watch out for brain-freeze because it'll be cold enough to — oh well, you get the picture.

Manhattan for the Mississippi

SERVES 4

⅔ cup bourbon whiskey

⅓ cup sweet vermouth

4 good shakes bitters

1 glug (or slug, to taste) Grand Marnier

Maraschino cherries, for garnish

Pour whiskey, vermouth, bitters and Grand Marnier in a cocktail shaker to small pitcher and blend well. Serve in cocktail glasses and garnish with a cherry.

If you triple this recipe, it may be stored in a 750 ml bottle in your freezer for future use.

MYC

Yellow Fever Cure

MAKES 8 SERVINGS

8   cups ice cubes, additional for serving

1   cup Southern Comfort

1   cup vodka

2   cups lime rum

1   cup triple sec

1   cup amaretto liqueur

1   cup Galliano liqueur

½   cup grenadine syrup

6   cups orange juice

Add ice cubes to a large glass jar; add all other ingredients, cover and shake to blend. Continue shaking until the jar has frosted a bit. Strain liquid into a pitcher and serve in ice-filled tumblers.

We are quite sure it is all the good vitamin C in this recipe that makes is so successfully "medicinal". If not that, the other ingredients will prevent your even caring if you are sick!

Doldrums Chasers

SERVES 32-36

1   (6-oz.) can frozen orange juice concentrate, thawed

1   (6-oz.) can frozen lemonade concentrate, thawed

¾   cup lemon juice

3   quarts lemon-lime soda, chilled

1   (750 ml) bottle Southern Comfort blended whiskey

    Sugar to taste

Combine concentrates and lemon juice. Add soda, then whiskey. Add sugar to taste.

Chill well before serving or pour over ice cubes made from juices or lemon-lime soda.

Memphis Blues Again

MAKES 1 DRINK

¾ oz. gin

¼ oz. vodka

¼ oz. blue curacao

   Splash(es) lime juice to taste

   Lime for garnish

Pour ingredients over ice and stir for one drink or to make 4 drinks, pour 3 oz. gin, 1 oz vodka and one of curacao over ice in a shaker... this is not a drink to drink alone. Garnish with slice of lime.

Sailing Witch's Party Punch

MAKES 12 SERVINGS

12 *cups ice cubes*

¾ *cup vodka*

¾ *cup raspberry schnapps*

¾ *cup melon liqueur (Midori)*

¼ *cup lime juice*

3 *cups sweet and sour mix*

1½ *cups club soda*

¼ *cup grenadine syrup*

Add ice cubes to a large glass jar and pour in vodka, schnapps, liqueur and lime juice. Shake jar to mix slightly. Pour in the sweet and sour mix, club soda and grenadine. Stir or shake jar to mix again.

To serve dip out ice cubes into a Collins glass and pour punch over them.

This spooky red and green punch is perfect for Halloween parties but will certainly bewitch your crew any time of the year.

Jones Orchard Daiquiri

MAKES 2 REGULAR SIZE, 1 KING SIZE

½   medium unpeeled fresh peach

1½ ozs. white rum

½   lime juice or juice of 1/2 lime

2   teaspoons sugar

½ to 1 cup crushed ice

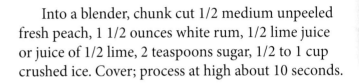

Into a blender, chunk cut 1/2 medium unpeeled fresh peach, 1 1/2 ounces white rum, 1/2 lime juice or juice of 1/2 lime, 2 teaspoons sugar, 1/2 to 1 cup crushed ice. Cover; process at high about 10 seconds.

Garnish with thick peach slice.

We guess you might enjoy fresh peaches from almost anywhere in this recipe, but we prefer to use the lovely produce from Jones Orchard in Millington near Memphis.

MYC

All Aboard for Appetizers!

Pier Party Pickled Shrimp

3 cups white vinegar

3 cups vegetable oil

1 cup olive oil

1 jar (1.5-ozs.) pickling spices

1 tablespoon kosher salt

2 tablespoons hot sauce

2 tablespoons celery seed

2½ tablespoons grated lemon zest

8 lbs. large shrimp, cooked, peeled and deveined

6 cups very thinly sliced onions

20 bay leaves

8 tablespoons capers

9 lemons, thinly sliced

In a large bowl, whisk together vinegar, vegetable oil, olive oil, pickling spices, salt, hot sauce, celery seed and lemon zest.

Place shrimp in a large container. Pour vinegar mixture over shrimp and mix well. Add sliced onions, bay leaves, capers and lemon slices to shrimp. Gently mix to combine. Cover well and refrigerate overnight.

Serve shrimp slightly chilled.

This is a great recipe for a big party, but it may be halved if necessary. If using frozen shrimp, thaw them according to package directions.

Tomato-Basil Dip

SERVES 6 TO 8

1   *cup mayonnaise*

½   *cup sour cream*

1   *tablespoon tomato paste*

½   *cup chopped fresh basil*

1   *tablespoon grated lemon zest*

Whisk together all ingredients until blended. Refrigerate in an airtight container until ready to serve.

This is a beautiful, fresh-tasting dip. Serve it with assorted fresh vegetables. It is especially good with crisp red and yellow bell pepper strips. Becasue it will hold well in the refrigerator for several days, it's great for impromptu entertaining.

Pickles²

SERVES 1 TO 50

2   quarts kosher dill pickles with garlic

3   cups sugar

1   cup vinegar

1   teaspoon mustard seed

1   teaspoon celery seed

15 whole cloves

Drain pickles and garlic, slice into rounds and place in a large mixing bowl. In a medium bowl, blend together sugar, vinegar, mustard and celery seed and cloves. Pour over sliced pickles and garlic. Let stand 24 hours, stirring occasionally.

Put pickle mixture in a clear screw-top jar and refrigerate.

These turn into a sweet and crunchy pickle that goes great with sandwiches and other summertime treats. The recipe lends itself to customization to personal taste.

Cobblestone Crunch

1½ lbs. assorted nuts

2 tablespoons chopped fresh rosemary

½ teaspoon cayenne pepper

1 tablespoon brown sugar

2 tablespoons coarse salt

1 tablespoon unsalted butter, melted

Preheat oven to 350 degrees.

Spread nuts on a baking sheet and toast for about 10 minutes. Stir frequently to prevent burning.

Meanwhile, combine remaining ingredients in a large bowl. Toss warm nuts with mixture and serve warm.

et tu, Brute! Dip

MAKES ABOUT 2 CUPS

2 cloves garlic, minced and mashed to a paste with

    ¼ teaspoon salt

1 tablespoon anchovy paste

2 tablespoons lemon juice

1 tablespoon Worcestershire sauce

1 teaspoon Dijon mustard

1 cup mayonnaise

½ cup grated Parmesan

Whisk together all ingredients and spoon into a serving dish.

Suggested dippers are celery and carrot sticks, romaine and endive leaves, blanched asparagus and green beans and multi-colored bell pepper strips. It's also wonderful with steamed shrimp.

The anchovy paste is what lends this its authentic "Caesar" flavor; it's quite subtle in this recipe. However, if you don't have any or simply don't like it, you may omit it and will still have a very good dip!

Treasure Olives

12 *ozs. kalamata olives*

    Zest of 1 lemon, finely grated

    Zest of 1 orange, finely grated

    Several sprigs of fresh rosemary, bruised

½ *cup extra virgin olive oil*

¼ *teaspoon crushed red pepper flakes*

1 *teaspoon fennel seed*

    Additional sprigs of fresh rosemary, for garnish

Place olives, lemon and orange zests, rosemary sprigs, olive oil, red pepper flakes and fennel seed in a saucepan and heat until the herbs sizzle. Remove from heat and let sit at room temperature for about 5 hours.

Before serving, remove the browned rosemary and add some fresh. Serve with additional sprigs of rosemary, if desired.

These olives will keep for 2 weeks in the refrigerator. Let them come to room temperature before serving.

Captain's Cucumber Dip

1   cucumber, peeled, seeded and finely chopped

     Kosher salt

6   green onions, white parts only, chopped

1   cup Greek yogurt

1   (3-oz.) package cream cheese, softened

2   tablespoons chopped fresh dill or 1 tablespoon dried
        dill weed

     Fresh dill sprigs or parsley, for garnish

Place chopped cucumber in a small colander; sprinkle lightly with salt and toss. Place colander over a bowl and refrigerate for 1 hour. Pat cucumber dry with paper towels and place in a medium mixing bowl. Add onion and set aside.

Place yogurt, cream cheese and dill in food processor or blender and process until smooth. Stir into cucumber mixture; cover and refrigerate at least one hour before serving.

Garnish as desired and serve with assorted fresh vegetables.

A dollop of this dip is also the perfect topping for grilled or smoked salmon.

Farmer's Market Sandwich Spread

10 SERVINGS

2   tomatoes, finely diced

1   cup finely chopped celery

1   small onion, finely diced

1   green bell pepper, finely diced

1   cucumber, peeled, seeded and finely diced

1   envelope plain geletin

1/4 cup cold water

1/4 cup boiling water

2   cups mayonnaise

1   teaspoon salt

Line a colander with paper towels and drain tomatoes, clelery, onion, bell pepper and cucumber thoroughly.

Meanwhile, soften gelatin in cold water, then stir in boiling water. Cool mixture and stir in mayonnaise and salt.

Add drained vegetables and stir well. Spoon mixture into a serving dish and refrigerate for 2 hours before serving.

Serve with assorted breads and crackers.

Shiver-Me-Timbers Chilled Shrimp

MAKES 6 SERVINGS

8	cups water
1	lime, halved
1	tablespoon salt
1	lb. medium shrimp in the shell, thawed if frozen
1	(14½-oz.) can Italian whole tomatoes
2	tablespoons fresh lime juice
⅓	cup finely diced celery
½	cup vodka
1	tablespoon Worcestershire sauce
1	tablespoon prepared horseradish
1	teaspoon Tabasco (more to taste)
½	teaspoon salt
1	teaspoon freshly ground black pepper
¼	cup finely chopped fresh cilantro
1	avocado, diced

In a large saucepan over high heat, bring the water to a boil. Squeeze in the juice of the lime and then add the lime to the water, along with the salt. When the water returns to a boil, add the shrimp in their shells. Cover the saucepan with a lid and remove it from the heat. Let the shrimp sit in the covered pan for 3 minutes; they will cook perfectly. When they are opaque, drain them and plunge them into an ice bath to stop the cooking. Peel the shrimp when they are cool enough to handle and refrigerate them until ready to assemble the dish.

Add whole tomatoes and their juice to a food processor bowl and process until a smooth sauce consistency is reached, about 10 seconds. Pour into a large bowl and add lime juice, celery, vodka, Worcestershire, horseradish, salt and pepper. Taste the sauce and adjust the seasonings as desired. Chill in the refrigerator for at least 2 hours to allow the flavors to meld.

To assemble, toss the chilled shrimp with the sauce. Add the cilantro and avocado and mix gently.

Spoon shrimp and sauce into large martini or margarita glasses and serve cold.

The sauce may be made 24 hours ahead, covered and refrigerated. Also, carefully follow the directions for cooking the shrimp as overcooking causes them to become rubbery in texture and just not as good!

First Mate's Ranch Dip (with cheese and bacon)

1   (16-oz.) container sour cream

1   (1-oz.) packet ranch dip mix

1   cup shredded Cheddar cheese

¼   cup crisply cooked and crumbled bacon

1   medium tomato, chopped, for garnish

Combine sour cream and dip mix; blend well. Stir in cheese and bacon. Cover and chill for 1 hour before serving. When ready to serve, sprinkle top of dip with diced tomatoes.

Serve with vegetable sticks or your favorite chips.

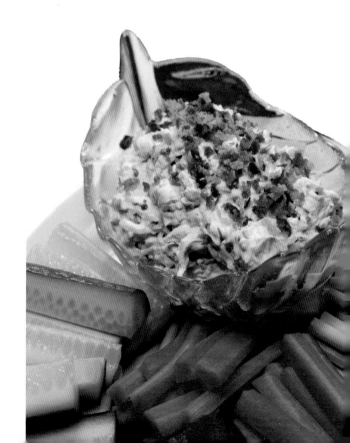

Potato Paddlewheels

MAKES 6 SERVINGS

4   large baking potatoes

½   stick butter, melted

8   slices bacon, cooked and crumbled

1   cup shredded Cheddar cheese

½   cup chopped green onion

Preheat oven to 400 degrees.

Scrub potatoes and cut into ½-inch slices. Brush both sides with butter and place slices on an ungreased baking sheet. Cook for 30-40 minutes or until lightly browned on both sides, turning once.

Meanwhile, stir together bacon, cheese and green onion in a small mixing bowl. When potato slices are done, top each with a spoonful of bacon mixture and return to the oven to continue baking until cheese is melted.

Serve warm potato slices with sour cream if desired.

Dried chives may be substituted for the green onion. Also, potato slices may be cooked in advance. When ready to serve, add cheese topping and microwave briefly to heat and melt the cheese.

Onions Overboard Snack Mix

MAKES ABOUT 9 CUPS

1 (6-oz.) can French fried onion rings

2 cups mixed nuts

1½ cups small pretzel twists

2 cans potato sticks

3 tablespoons butter, melted

3 tablespoons spicy brown mustard

Combine onions, nuts, pretzels and potato sticks in a 4-quart microwave-safe bowl. Whisk together butter and mustard. Pour over mixture in bowl and toss well to coat evenly. Spread paper towels on a baking sheet and set aside.

Microwave snack mix, uncovered, on high for 6 minutes, stirring mixture every 2 minutes. Transfer mixture to prepared baking sheet and allow to cool completely. Store in an airtight container.

Rebel Reuben Spread

SERVES 8

2 packages deli-style corned beef slices, coarsely chopped

1 (14 oz.) can shredded sauerkraut, drained, rinsed and chopped

1 tablespoon finely chopped onion

2 cups mayonanaise

1 cup shredded Swiss cheese

Prehead oven to 350 degrees. Spray an 8 x 8-inch baking dish with cooking spray and set aside.

In a medium mixing bowl, mix all ingredients well. Spoon mixture into prepared pan and bake for 35 minutes; until dish is heated through and cheese is melted

Serve with assorted crackers or pieces of toasted rye or pumpernickel bread for an authentic twist.

Greek Sailor's Cheese Dice

MAKES 6 SERVINGS

10   ozs. feta cheese, cut into 1/2-inch cubes

½   cup extra virgin olive oil

3   tablespoons fresh lemon juice

2   cloves garlic, thinly sliced

½   teaspoon dried oregano

¼   teaspoon crushed red pepper flakes

   Pita bread, cut into wedges

Mix cheese cubes, olive oil, lemon juice, garlic, oregano and red pepper in a large zip top plastic bag. Chill at least 2 hours or overnight. Place feta cubes in a serving bowl and serve with the pita wedges.

This can be made up to 1 week ahead and kept covered in the refrigerator. For a really impressive presentation, serve cheese with an assortment of olives and some icy cold ouzo, a licorice-flavored liqueur from Greece.

Ripley Bruschetta

SERVES 8

1   loaf baguette bread, cut on diagonal into 1/2-inch slices

7   oz. soft goat cheese or fresh mozzarella

3   fresh and worthy tomatoes, finely chopped and drained

1   small red onion, finely chopped

Lightly toast baguette slices. Spread with cheese and top each with 1 tablespoon of tomato and 1 teaspoon of onion. Serve immediately.

Place the chopped tomatoes in a colander and salt them very lightly to help promote complete draining. Adding a bit of chopped fresh basil is a nice touch and fresh, home-grown tomatoes are a MUST in this recipe!

Channel Chip Cheese Treats

MAKES 24 "COOKIES"

1   stick butter, softened

1   cup grated sharp Cheddar cheese

Dash of Tabasco sauce

2   cups all-purpose flour

1/2 cup crushed potato chips

1/2 cup chopped pecans, optional

Finely shredded Parmesan

Paprika

Preheat oven to 350 degrees.

Combine butter, Cheddar, Tabasco, flour, crushed chips and pecans, if using. Form dough into 1 1/2-inch balls. Place on a parchment-lined baking sheet and press each down with the back side of a fork, scoring twice in opposite directions.

Sprinkle with Parmesan and top with paprika. Bake about 18 minutes until edges are browned. Cool completely on a rack and store in an airtight container.

Big Batch Boat Fare

Italian Beef Submarines

MAKES ABOUT 10 HEARTY SANDWICHES

3   cups water

1   teaspoon salt

1   teaspoon ground black pepper

1   teaspoon dried oregano

1   teaspoon dried basil

1   teaspoon onion salt

1   teaspoon dried parsley

1   teaspoon garlic powder

1   bay leaf

1   (.7-oz.) package dry Italian-style salad dressing mix

1   (5-lb.) rump roast

Optional

    Prosciutto

    Fresh spinach leaves

    Various cheeses

Combine water with salt, pepper, oregano, basil onion salt, parsley, garlic powder, bay leaf and salad dressing mix in a medium saucepan. Stir well to blend and bring mixture to a boil.

Place roast in slow cooker and pour warm salad dressing mixture over it. Cover and cook on Low for 10 to 12 hours or on High for 4 to 5 hours. When roast reaches desired doneness, remove it to a platter and slice the meat or shred with a fork. Serve on sandwich rolls.

To make these really special, offer roasted red peppers, grilled onions, fresh spinach leaves, prosciutto and a variety of cheese slices along with the traditional mustard and mayonnaise to customize each sandwich.

Water Wings—Buffalo Style

MAKES ABOUT 10 SPICY SANDWICHES

7   boneless, skinless chicken breast halves

2   (17.5-fluid oz.) bottles Buffalo wing sauce, divided

1   (1-oz.) package dry ranch salad dressing mix

4   tablespoons butter, melted

10 hoagie rolls, split lengthwise

Place chicken breasts in slow cooker and add one bottle of the wing sauce; sprinkle with ranch dressing mix.

Cover and cook on Low for 6 to 7 hours. When chicken is done, stir in butter. Remove chicken pieces to a platter or cutting board and shred the meat finely with two forks.

To serve, pile the meat on hoagie rolls and splash each one with the additional wing sauce. Add onions, pickles, or cole slaw to give the sandwich an extra dimension of flavor and a satisfying crunchiness.

Easy and spicy and much more simple to serve and enjoy than traditional hot wings.

Chuckwagon Burger

MAKES 8 BURGERS

2   lbs. ground chuck

½   cup chopped onion

1   cup cracker crumbs

2   cloves garlic, crushed

1   egg, lightly beaten

1   teaspoon pepper

½   teaspoon salt

½   cup steak sauce

Mix all ingredients and shape into eight patties at least ¾-inch thick. Fry in a heavy skillet or grill to medium-well or desired doneness. Serve on toasted buns and offer the usual burger toppings.

MYC

Flotilla Tortillas (Tex-Mex BBQ)

FEEDS ABOUT 10 HUNGRY SAILORS

2   (8-ounce) cans tomato sauce

1¼ cups barbeque sauce

2   medium white onions, chopped

2-3 (4-ounce) cans diced green chilies

¼   cup chili powder (more to taste)

1¼ teaspoons ground cumin

1¼ teaspoons dried oregano

¼   teaspoon ground cinnamon

3½ to 4-pounds boneless pork loin roast, trimmed

¾   cup chopped fresh cilantro

3   dozen tortillas or taco shells

In bowl of slow cooker, mix tomato sauce, barbeque sauce, onion, green chilies, chili powder, cumin, oregano and cinnamon. Place pork roast in cooker and spoon sauce over it.

Cover and cook on Low for 8 to 10 hours or until pork is very tender. Remove roast to a cutting board and using two forks, pull meat into shreds. Pour sauce into a large serving dish and stir in shredded pork and fresh cilantro.

This is certainly not the barbeque we "grew up on" in the Midsouth. However, when served in taco shells or tortillas along with some shredded lettuce, it will definitely earn a spot of its own in the history of pulled pork!

Outer Banks Brunswick Stew

MAKES 8 SERVINGS

1   tablespoon vegetable oil

1   pound country-style pork ribs

1   large onion, chopped

1   roasted chicken, deboned and shredded

1   (28-oz.) can diced tomatoes

¾   cup ketchup

¾   cup steak sauce

½   cup cider vinegar

2   tablespoons Worcestershire sauce

1   tablespoon hot sauce

     Juice of 1 lemon

2   chicken bouillon cubes

½   tablespoon ground black pepper

1   (15-oz.) can whole kernel corn, undrained

1   cup frozen lima beans, thawed

Heat vegetable oil in a skillet over medium heat and brown ribs on all sides. Transfer to a slow cooker. Place onion in the skillet and cook until tender; add them to the slow cooker along with the shredded chicken.

In a mixing bowl, stir together tomatoes, ketchup, steak sauce, vinegar, Worcestershire, hot sauce, lemon juice, chicken bouillon and black pepper. Pour sauce over ingredients in slow cooker, cover and cook on High for 6 hours.

Remove ribs, discard bones and shred the meat before returning it to the slow cooker. Mix in corn and lima beans; cover and continue cooking for 2 more hours on High.

Although this may seem like a lot of work, anyone who has ever traveled in the southeast, especially the Carolinas, has probably enjoyed a dish of this wonderful "regional" stew. Serve it with some warm crusty bread and it becomes a meal-in-a-bowl.

Rustic River Stew

Makes 12 servings

3   pounds beef stew meat

     Salt and pepper to taste

2   tablespoons vegetable oil, divided

2   (14-oz.) cans beef broth

1   (10.5-oz.) can beef consommé

2   cups Burgundy wine

1   cup water

1   teaspoon ground mustard (dry)

1   teaspoon dried thyme

5   red potatoes, cut into chunks

½   pound baby carrots

½   pound pearl onions, peeled

1   cup frozen green peas

Season beef with salt and pepper and brown in batches, in vegetable oil over medium heat until evenly browned, adding additional oil as needed. Drain meat and set aside.

In a slow cooker, mix beef broth, consommé, wine, water, dry mustard and thyme. Place beef into the mixture and add potatoes, carrots and onions. Add the green peas at the end of the cooking cycle, they'll take no more than 10 minutes to become infused with the stew.

Cover and cook 6 hours on Low or 4 hours on High.

Browning the meat in batches allows for a more thorough, crispy browning. Crowding all the meat into the skillet at one time causes it to steam more than brown and the results are not nearly so flavorful. If you prefer a thicker stew, toss the seasoned beef with all-purpose flour before browning. It will thicken the liquid as it cooks and you won't have to worry about "lumps" from adding flour or cornstarch at the end of cooking time.

South Padre Island Taco Soup

MAKES 12 SERVINGS

1½ lbs. ground beef

2   medium white onions, chopped

2   (16-oz.) cans chili beans, with liquid

1   (15-oz.) can kidney beans, with liquid

2   (15-oz.) cans whole kernel corn, with liquid

2   (8-oz.) cans tomato sauce

3   cups water

3   (14.5-oz.) cans peeled and diced tomatoes

1-2 (4-oz.) cans diced green chilies, drained

2   (1.25-oz.) packages taco seasoning mix

In a large skillet, cook ground beef until browned over medium heat. Drain well on paper towels.

Place ground beef and all remaining ingredients in a large slow cooker and stir well to blend. Cover and cook on Low for 8 hours. Serve with Tasty Tortilla Strips (recipe follows).

Tasty Tortilla Strips

2   dozen (or so) corn tortillas

Vegetable oil

Preheat oven to 400 degrees.

Lightly brush both sides of tortillas with oil. Cut tortillas into strips and place in a single layer on baking sheets. Bake until crisp, about 10 to 15 minutes. Serve with any Tex-Mex soups for an authentic touch.

MYC

Rio Grande Chicken Soup

MAKES 8 SERVINGS

1   *lb. cooked chicken, shredded*

1   *(15-oz.) can whole peeled tomatoes, mashed*

1   *(10-ounce) can enchilada sauce*

1   *medium onion, chopped*

1   *(4-oz.) can chopped green chilies*

2   *cloves garlic, minced*

2   *cups water*

1   *(14.5-oz.) can chicken broth*

1   *teaspoon cumin*

1   *teaspoon chili powder*

1   *teaspoon salt*

¼   *teaspoon ground black pepper*

1   *bay leaf*

1   *(10-oz.) package frozen corn*

1   *tablespoon chopped fresh cilantro*

Place chicken, tomatoes, enchilada sauce, onion, green chilies and garlic in the slow cooker. Pour in water and chicken broth and season with cumin, chili powder, salt, pepper and bay leaf. Stir in corn and cilantro.

Cover and cook on Low for 6 to 8 hours or on High for 3 to 4 hours. Serve with Tasty Tortilla Strips (pg 165), a dollop of sour cream and a squeeze of lime.

Chickasaw Corn Chowder

MAKES 8 SERVINGS

5   potatoes, peeled and cubed

2   medium onions, chopped

1¾ cups diced cooked ham

3   celery stalks, chopped

1   (15.25-oz.) can whole kernel corn, undrained

2   tablespoons margarine

    Salt and pepper to taste

2   chicken bouillon cubes

1   (12-oz.) can evaporated milk

In a slow cooker, place the potatoes, onion, ham, celery, corn, margarine and salt and pepper. Add enough water to cover the mixture and drop in the bouillon cubes.

Cover and cook on Low for 8 to 9 hours; stir in evaporated milk and continue cooking an additional 30 minutes.

Yankee White Bean & Bacon Chowder

MAKES 8 SERVINGS

2   cups dried great northern beans, picked and rinsed

2⅔ cups water

8   slices bacon

2   medium carrots, peeled and chopped

2   celery stalks, chopped

1   large onion, chopped

2   medium potatoes, peeled and cubed

1¼ teaspoons Italian seasoning

⅛ teaspoon ground black pepper

4   (14.5-oz.) cans low-sodium chicken broth

1⅓ cups milk

Place beans in a large bowl; add water. Cover and allow to soak overnight; drain and rinse when ready to use.

In a large skillet, over medium heat, fry bacon until crispy. Drain on paper towels, crumble and set aside.

In a slow cooker, combine the carrot, celery, onion, potato, Italian seasoning, black pepper and reserved beans and bacon. Add chicken broth. Cover and cook on Low for 7 1/2 to 9 hours or until beans are tender.

Working with about 2 cups at a time, puree mixture until smooth. Return all to the slow cooker and stir in the milk. Cover and cook on High until heated through.

Originally called "Northern White Bean & Bacon Chowder", we just had to take certain "liberties" in renaming this recipe!

Tasty Soup for a Big Group

MAKES 12 SERVINGS

1   cup chopped celery

1   cup chopped carrot

½   cup chopped onion

1   tablespoon butter

10   cups water

2½   cups dried split peas , or lentils rinsed

2   cups cubed fully cooked ham

2   teaspoons salt

1   teaspoon dried marjoram

½   teaspoon ground black pepper

In a large skillet, sauté celery, carrot and onion in butter for 3 to 4 minutes, or until crisp-tender. In a 5-quart slow cooker, combine water, split peas (or lentils), ham, salt, marjoram and pepper. Stir in the celery mixture.

Cover and cook on Low for 4 hours or until peas (or lentils) are tender.

Most Americans are familiar with this soup made with dried peas, it is also delicious with lentils. Long a staple in kitchens throughout Europe and much of the Middle East, lentils are a great source of iron and serve as a meat substitute for many. Brown lentils are the most common in the United States and are available at most supermarkets now. In addition to various nutrients, they add a heartiness and nice texture to this soup.

A&P Vichyssoise (Asparagus/Potato)

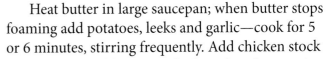

MAKES 12 SERVINGS OR A MEAL FOR 8

3   tablespoons butter

6   medium Yukon potatoes, peeled and diced

2   leeks, trimmed and sliced in
     thin rounds

1   large clove garlic, minced
     fresh thyme sprig

6   cups chicken stock

1½   lbs. asparagus, trimmed
     and cut into 1-inch lengths.

2   tablespoons good quality
     white wine vinegar

     Salt and pepper to taste

½   cup sour cream

*Optional: ½ teaspoon fresh dill,
plus extra for garnish; or 2
tablespoons fresh mint, plus
extra for garnish.*

Heat butter in large saucepan; when butter stops foaming add potatoes, leeks and garlic—cook for 5 or 6 minutes, stirring frequently. Add chicken stock and bring to a boil. Reduce heat to simmer, add asparagus and cook until all vegetables are tender, about 10 minutes. (Remove and set aside several asparagus tips and leek rounds for garnish.)

After mixture has cooled sufficiently to handle, blend in batches in a food processor or blender until smooth.

Serve hot or chilled with a dollop of sour cream. Garnish variously with dill, mint, asparagus tips and leek rounds.

Adding mint is especially pleasing in the chilled version.

MYC

Swab-the-Bowl Vegetable Beef Soup

MAKES 10 SERVINGS

1 lb. ground beef

1 (46-oz.) can tomato juice

1 (16-oz.) package frozen mixed vegetables, thawed

2 cups frozen cubed hash brown potatoes, thawed

1 envelope dry onion soup mix

Worcestershire sauce to taste

Ground black pepper to taste

In a large skillet, cook beef over medium heat until no longer pink. Drain well and transfer to the bowl of a 5-quart slow cooker. Stir in tomato juice, vegetables, potatoes and soup mix and blend well. Add Worcestershire and pepper as desired.

Cover and cook on Low for 8 to 10 hours.

Nothing could be easier than "throwing together" a batch of this traditional veggie soup. Convenience products replace time spent chopping everything and the slow cooking develops the flavors as nicely as if it had been simmered on the stove top for hours.

Red Chili Tonight, Sailor's Delight

MAKES 12-14 SERVINGS

2   lbs. ground beef

1   cup chopped yellow onion

2   garlic cloves, minced

2   (16-oz.) cans dark red kidney beans, rinsed and drained

2   (14.5-oz.) cans stewed tomatoes, coarsely chopped

1   (15-oz.) can pizza sauce

1   (4-oz.) can chopped green chilies

4   teaspoons chili powder (more to taste)

1   teaspoon dried basil

½   teaspoon salt

⅛   teaspoon ground black pepper

In a Dutch oven, cook beef, onion and garlic over medium heat until meat is no longer pink. Drain well and transfer to a 5-quart slow cooker; stir in remaining ingredients.

Cover and cook on Low for 6 hours.

This classic short-cut chili gets a unique twist by using pizza sauce instead of plain tomato sauce, along with a touch of basil. Complete with a winning presentation by serving the dish garnished with a variety of peppers and some chopped cilantro.

Oh Black Chili, Keep on Rollin'*

MAKES 8 SERVINGS

3   *lbs. boneless pork, cut into 1/2-inch cubes*

2   *tablespoons vegetable oil, divided*

4   *(15.5-oz.) cans black beans, drained and rinsed*

2   *cups chopped onion*

2   *cups chopped yellow bell pepper*

2   *cups thick-and-chunky salsa*

2   *(15-oz.) cans canned diced tomatoes*

4   *garlic cloves, minced*

2   *teaspoons chili powder*

1   *teaspoon cumin*

½   *teaspoon crushed red pepper*

    Sour cream, shredded cheese, for garnish

In a large skillet, lightly brown pork cubes in oil. Brown in batches, adding more oil as needed. Drain well on paper towels and transfer to the bowl of a slow cooker.

Combine all remaining ingredients, except garnishes; cover and cook on Low for 7 to 8 hours. When serving, top individual bowls with sour cream and cheese as desired.

With sincerest apologies to a Mud Island Amphitheatre crowd favorite, The Doobie Brothers! "Oh, Blackwater, keep on rollin', Mississippi moon won't you keep on shinin' on me…"

Whitecap Chili

MAKES 8 SERVINGS

¾   lb. boneless, skinless chicken breasts, cubed

1   medium onion, chopped

1   red bell pepper, chopped or ½ cup smoked red pepper

1   tablespoon canola oil

1   garlic clove, minced

1½ cups water

1   (15-oz.) can whole tomatoes, drained, seeded and chopped

1   (15-oz.) can white kidney or cannellini beans, rinsed and drained

1   (15-oz.) can garbanzo beans (chickpeas), rinsed and drained

1   (11-oz.) can whole kernel white corn or 1¼ cups frozen corn

1   (4-oz.) can diced green chilies

1-2 teaspoons chicken bouillon granules

1   teaspoon ground cumin

In a large skillet, sauté chicken and onion in oil until onion is tender. Add garlic and cook 1 minute longer, Transfer to the bowl of a slow cooker and stir in remaining ingredients.

Cover and cook on Low for 5 to 6 hours, making sure chicken is cooked through.

Garbanzo beans amp up the texture in this chili option. Who would have thought?

Up from the Gulf Red Beans and Rice

MAKES 8 SERVINGS

1   lb. dried red beans, soaked overnight

10 cups water

1   pound andouille sausage, sliced into rounds

1   large sweet onion, chopped

1   green bell pepper, chopped

1   jalapeno pepper, seeded and chopped, optional

8   garlic cloves, chopped

1   teaspoon ground black pepper

1   teaspoon Creole seasoning, or to taste

6   fresh basil leaves, chopped

1   ham hock

4   cups cooked white rice

Drain and rinse beans well after soaking overnight. Add beans and 10 cups of water to slow cooker. Heat a skillet over medium-high heat. Brown the sausage in the skillet; remove with a slotted spoon and transfer to the slow cooker, reserving drippings in the skillet.

Add onion, green pepper, jalapeno and garlic to the drippings; cook and stir until tender, about 5 minutes. Transfer all skillet ingredients to the slow cooker.

Season the mixture with pepper and Creole seasoning. Add the fresh basil and ham hock. Cover and cook on Low for about 8 hours, or until the beans are tender. If the mixture seems to thin after the cooking time, remove the lid and adjust heat to High to cook until they reach the desired texture.

To serve, place a 1/2 cup mound of rice in the center of each serving bowl, and spoon beans around it.

Although both native to Louisiana, Creole and Cajun cooking are not the same. This recipe is an example of Creole cuisine which, today, reflects the full-flavored combination of the best of French, Spanish and African influences.

Cajun cooking, on the other hand, is more "country-style" and robust, blending French traditions with Southern style and food availability. The following recipe is considered classic Cajun fare.

Show Me Your Jambalaya!!

MAKES 12 SERVINGS

1   pound boneless, skinless chicken breasts, cut into 1-inch cubes

1   pound andouille sausage, sliced

2   tablespoons vegetable oil

1   (28-ounce) can diced tomatoes, with liquid

1   large onion, chopped

1   large bell pepper, chopped

1   cup chopped celery

1   cup chicken broth

2   teaspoons dried oregano

2   teaspoons dried parsley

2   teaspoons Cajun seasoning

1   teaspoon cayenne pepper (or to taste)

½   teaspoon dried thyme

1   pound frozen cooked shrimp without tails

6   lemons or limes

In a large skillet over medium-high heat, lightly brown chicken and sausage in oil. Transfer meat to a slow cooker and add all ingredients except shrimp. Cover and cook 7 to 8 hours on Low or 3 to 4 hours on High. Stir in shrimp during the last 30 minutes of the cooking time and be sure they are heated through before serving. Serve with lemon or lime slices.

This is a relatively quick and easy way to prepare a delicious dish that often takes much more time and hands-on effort to prepare. However, the long, slow cooking produces a genuine taste of Mardi Gras without some of the "trappings"!!

Pegleg's New Year's Peas

MAKES 6 TO 8 SERVINGS

1   lb. black-eyed peas, soaked overnight

1   onion, chopped

1   stalk celery, chopped

1   red bell pepper, chopped

2   garlic cloves, minced

1   smoked ham hock

32 ozs. low-sodium chicken stock

1   bay leaf

4-5 cups cooked white rice

    Hot pepper sauce

Drain and rinse peas and add to slow cooker; add onion, celery, bell pepper, garlic and ham hock. Pour in chicken stock and stir to combine ingredients. Submerge bay leaf into the mixture.

Cover and cook on Low for 7 to 8 hours or until peas are tender. Discard ham hock and bay leaf. To serve, spoon white rice into a bowl and ladle peas over the top. Pass hot sauce so each diner may season the dish to personal tastes.

Southern tradition dictates that this dish (usually known as Hoppin' John) be served the first thing on New Year's Day to ensure good luck in the coming year. We may not have been all that "lucky" through the years, but just think of the mess we might be in without it!

Optional ingredients to stir in might include cooked collard greens and bite size chunks of smoky ham...yum, yum.

Oktoberfeast

MAKES 8 SERVINGS

2   tablespoons vegetable oil

2   lbs. kielbasa, cut into ¼-inch slices

1   medium apple, diced

1   large onion, diced

2   garlic cloves, minced

2   (12-oz.) bottles beer

½   cup honey mustard

1   tablespoon sugar

1   bay leaf

1   (2-lb.) bag fresh sauerkraut, rinsed and drained

    Black pepper, to taste

    Caraway seeds, optional

In a large skillet over medium high heat, saute kielbasa until crispy. Remove with a slotted spoon to the bowl of slow cooker, reserving drippings in skillet.

Return skillet to high heat momentarily and splash in ¼ cup of beer to deglaze. Turn heat under skillet down to medium, add apple, onion and garlic and cook, stirring until lightly browned. Add to slow cooker with kielbasa and add beer, mustard, sugar and bay leaf. Stir to mix well and add sauerkraut, stirring again.

Cook on Low for 5 to 6 hours or until sausage is tender and mixture is hot through.

Dished up with some fresh rye or pumpernickel bread, this is a tasty way to celebrate Fall. And if you must do something with the rest of that case of beer you bought to make this dish, well, that's just one you take for the team.

Cool Salads for Hot Times

Barge Hand's Salad

MAKES 10 SERVINGS

2½ *pounds boneless sirloin steak, about 1-inch thick*

½ *cup plus 2 tablespoons cider vinegar*

¼ *cup plus 1 tablespoon olive oil*

¼ *cup soy sauce*

7½ *cups cooked cubed potatoes*

1¼ *cups diced green bell pepper*

½ *cup chopped green onion*

¼ *cup minced fresh parsley*

½ *cup bottled Caesar salad dressing*

Place steak in a large zip-top bag or shallow glass container. Combine vinegar, oil and soy sauce and pour over the steak. Seal bag or cover dish and marinate for at least 1 hour or overnight. Drain, discarding marinade.

Grill or broil steak for 8 to 10 minutes or until meat reaches desired doneness. Slice, across the grain, into thin strips and place in large salad bowl. Add potatoes, bell pepper, onion and parsley. Pour in dressing and toss lightly to coat.

If your crowd likes its steak rare, you can substitute flank steak for the sirloin, but flank steak becomes quite tough when cooked beyond rare. Meat thermometers are valuable tools to have anywhere you plan to cook. For this recipe, the thermometer should read 145 degrees for medium rare; 160 degrees for medium and 170 degrees for well done. Insert probe in center of the meat and away from bones if you are cooking poultry or other meats with bones.

Gilligan's Good Salad

MAKES 14 SERVINGS (7 IF STRANDED ON A DESERT ISLE..)

¾ cup vegetable oil

¼ cup fresh lemon juice

2 garlic cloves, minced

½ teaspoon salt

½ teaspoon pepper

2 heads romaine lettuce, rinsed, dried and torn into bite-size
    pieces

2 cups chopped tomato

1 cup shredded Swiss cheese

⅔ cup toasted slivered almonds

½ cup grated Parmesan

8 slices bacon, cooked and crumbled

1 cup Caesar salad croutons

In a jar with a tight-fitting lid, combine oil, lemon juice, garlic, salt and pepper; cover and shake well to blend. Chill dressing while making salad.

In a large bowl, toss together romaine, tomatoes, Swiss cheese, almonds, Parmesan and bacon.

When ready to serve, shake dressing vigorously, pour over salad and toss well. Top with croutons immediately before serving.

Cranky Wench Pasta Salad

MAKES 12 SERVINGS

2½ cups farfalle pasta

¾ cup mayonnaise

¾ cup sour cream

3 tablespoons cider vinegar

2 tablespoons Dijon-style mustard

1½ teaspoons granulated sugar

¾ teaspoon ground black pepper

¼ teaspoon dried dill weed

¼ teaspoon salt

3 cups seedless green grapes, halved

3 cups diced ham or cooked chicken

¾ cup chopped green onions

2¼ cups sharp Cheddar cheese cubes

Cook pasta in a large pot of lightly salted water until al dente. Drain and rinse with cold water. Set aside.

In a small bowl, mix together mayonnaise, sour cream, vinegar, mustard, sugar, pepper, dill weed and salt.

In a large bowl, combine pasta, grapes, ham, green onions and cheese. Toss with dressing; cover and chill overnight or at least 6 hours before serving.

Food is not actually gender-specific so, in reality, the men could have this salad, too, if they so desire. However, in case they think it is "too sissy" for them, a cooler full of the Barge Hand's Salad might be the way to go for "the boys".

Parrothead's Potpourri

MAKES 10 SERVINGS

2   *heads leaf lettuce or 1 lb. spinach, rinsed, dried and torn into bite-size pieces*

13   *oz. fresh strawberries, sliced*

13   *oz. fresh blueberries*

1   *yellow or orange pepper, sliced thin*

⅓   *cup toasted slivered almonds*

⅓   *cup chopped red onion*

Optional:

2   *mangoes, peeled and cut into strips*

7   *slices bacon*

Toss lettuce, strawberries, blueberries, mango, peppers, almonds and onion together in a large salad bowl. Cover and refrigerate at least 30 minutes, but no more than 3 hours before serving.

Cook bacon in a large skillet over medium-high heat, turning occasionally, until crisp and evenly browned, about 10 minutes. Drain bacon on paper towels, then crumble and sprinkle over salad immediately before serving.

The title of this recipe? Well, if you are one there is no need to explain and if you aren't one there's no way to explain!

Confetti Corn Concoction

MAKES 10 SERVINGS

2½   cups fresh sweet corn kernels

¾   cup chopped tomato

½   cup chopped green bell pepper

½   cup chopped celery

¼   cup chopped onion

¼   cup prepared Ranch salad dressing

Combine all vegetables in a large bowl. Add dressing and toss well to blend. Cover and refrigerate until serving time.

This beautiful dish is great in summer when all the fresh corn is in season. Serve it with grilled meats or your favorite fish recipe.

MYC

1001 Island Salad Dressing

MAKES 2 26-OUNCE JARS

1   (8-oz.) package cream cheese, softened

1   (5-oz.) jar pimento cheese spread

1   (14-oz.) can condensed tomato soup

2   cups salad dressing (Miracle Whip)

¼   cup sugar

1   small onion, grated

2   garlic cloves, minced

½   cup white vinegar

½-¾ cup vegetable oil

    salt and freshly ground black pepper, to taste

Blend cream cheese and pimento spread; stir in soup and salad dressing. Using an electric mixer or blender, mix in sugar, onion, garlic and vinegar until well-blended.

With mixer or blender on low, slowly drizzile in oil and mix until it is incorporated.

Add salt and pepper to taste. Pour dressing into glass jars, cover and refrigerate.

Since this makes such a large amount, it is great for gifts and sharing.

Popeye Salad with Olive Oyl Dressing

MAKES 12 SERVINGS

¼ cup chopped Vidalia onion

¼ cup cider vinegar

¼ cup honey

¾ teaspoon Dijon mustard

⅓ cup plus 2 tablespoons olive oil

¾ teaspoon poppy seeds

12 cups fresh baby spinach leaves

8 slices bacon, cooked and crumbled

1 medium Vidalia onion, thinly sliced and separated into rings

Optional:

1 ear freshly picked sweet corn

To make dressing, combine chopped onion, vinegar, honey and mustard in a blender or food processor; cover and process until smooth. While processing, slowly add oil in a steady stream to incorporate. Stir in poppy seeds.

In a large bowl, toss spinach, bacon and onion rings. Serve with dressing.

Croutons and thinly sliced hard-cooked eggs may be added at serving time, if desired. And if you can get an ear of freshly picked, sweet corn, cut the curnels from the cob and add them to the salad.

A Floating Garden

MAKES 10 SERVINGS

1   head fresh broccoli, chopped

1   head fresh cauliflower, chopped

⅓   cup chopped onion

1   small can chopped black olives, drained

12 button mushrooms, sliced

1   (4-oz.) jar diced pimentos

1   (16-oz.) bottle oil and vinegar salad dressing

2   tablespoons granulated sugar

    Salt to taste

1   teaspoon ground black pepper

In a large salad bowl, combine broccoli, cauliflower, onion, olives, mushrooms and pimentos. Stir to mix.

Meanwhile, combine salad dressing, sugar, salt and pepper. Whisk well to blend. Pour over salad and toss well. Cover and refrigerate until ready to serve.

This colorful and tasty salad may be made as much as 24 hours prior to serving.

Fish-Fry Slaw

MAKES 10 SERVINGS

⅓ cup vinegar

3 tablespoons vegetable oil

2 teaspoons garlic salt

3 teaspoons sugar

¾ teaspoon dried tarragon

8½ cups shredded cabbage

In a small bowl or jar with a tight-fitting lid, combine vinegar, oil, garlic salt, sugar and tarragon. Shake jar well to blend mixture.

Place cabbage in a large bowl; add dressing and toss to coat. Cover and refrigerate before serving.

This crisp, fresh-tasting slaw will hold in the refrigerator for about a week IF you have any leftovers…but don't count on it. Stir in some yellow mustard and you have a great slaw to accompany bar-b-que or hot dogs.

Simply Antipasto

MAKES 10 SERVINGS

7½ cups torn lettuce leaves

10 oz. hard salami, julienned

½ pound provolone cheese, julienned

1¼ cups shredded mozzarella

3 medium tomatoes, chopped

2 (6-oz.) cans ripe olives, drained and halved

4 teaspoons minced chives

1½ cups tomato sauce

½ cup vegetable oil

¼ cup cider vinegar

1½ teaspoons sugar

1 teaspoon salt

1½ teaspoons dried oregano

½ teaspoon garlic powder

¼ teaspoon ground black pepper

Place lettuce in the bottom of a large serving bowl. Arrange salami, cheeses, tomatoes and olives over the top.

Meanwhile, combine chives, tomato sauce, oil, vinegar, sugar, salt, oregano, garlic powder and black pepper in a blender or food processor. Cover and process until mixture is smooth. Drizzle over chilled salad when ready to serve.

This "deconstructed" antipasto platter is easier to prepare and to serve than the traditional one. Think of this as a pizza explosion and the crust went overboard, taking lots of carbs with it!

Potatoes in Paradise

MAKES 8 SERVINGS

3   lbs. baby red potatoes, cut in half

1   cup olive oil, divided

5   garlic cloves, minced, divided

1   tablespoon seafood seasoning

8   oz. bacon

¼   cup balsamic vinegar

    Salt and ground black pepper, to taste

1   large red onion, coarsely chopped

1   bunch parsley, minced

5   hard-cooked eggs, coarsely chopped

Preheat oven to 350 degrees.

Toss halved potatoes with 1/2 cup olive oil, 3 cloves of minced garlic and seafood seasoning. Place in a single layer on baking sheets and roast in preheated oven until tender and browned, about 30 to 40 minutes. Once cooked, remove from oven and set aside to cool slightly.

Meanwhile, place bacon in a large, deep skillet. Cook over medium heat until evenly browned and crispy. Pour off bacon drippings and reserve. When bacon is cool, crumble and set aside.

Whisk together balsamic vinegar, 2 cloves of minced garlic, salt and pepper in a large bowl. Pour the oil in a slow, steady stream while whisking vigorously to make a vinaigrette. Toss the roasted potatoes with the dressing, adding the reserved bacon drippings. Fold in bacon, red onion, parsley and eggs. Allow to stand at room temperature about 20 minutes before serving.

This is decadent! And the good news is, it is a way to avoid having to use so much mayonnaise-based food in an environment where refrigeration may be limited.

BLT Salad Wrap

MAKES ABOUT 8 WRAPS

6   cups torn romaine lettuce leaves

2   medium tomatoes, chopped

⅔   cup cooked and crumbled bacon

½   cup Caesar salad dressing

2   cups freshly shredded Parmesan

8   (10-inch) flour tortillas

Combine lettuce, tomato, bacon and salad dressing in a large bowl; add cheese and toss well to combine ingredients.

Spoon mixture evenly onto tortillas and roll up burrito-style. Wrap sandwiches in waxed paper or plastic wrap and refrigerate until serving time.

Many of your favorite salads will convert well to a wrap, making them easy to serve and handle while onboard. Use your imagination to create interesting combinations of veggies, meats and cheeses that will treat and surprise your guests.

To make a wrap, place tortilla on a flat surface and add filling to the center, leaving room on all sides. Fold up the bottom first, then turn each side to the center and…viola!...that's a wrap!

Index

ACKNOWLEDGEMENTS

The club is indebted to everyone whose work, insight and recollections made this book possible. Special thanks to Bob Schwartz and to his father, who took so many of the spectacular photographs that brought this book to life. Thanks as well to Demetra Gordon, Charles Cook, Mary Margarite Buck, Henry Ellis, Ham Smythe, Norman Blackley, Sandy Coles, Roy Hendrix, Helen Georgi, John Hill, & Keith Brown.

AND THE PUBLISHING COMMITTEE EXPRESSES ITS APPRECIATION TO THE FOLLOWING FRIENDS AND MEMBERS WHOSE FINANCIAL SUPPORT WAS INSTRUMENTAL TO THE BOOK'S PRODUCTION:

COMMODORES:

The Family of Charles Postal Brown   *Chickasaw IV*

John & Patricia Hill   *Evening Star*

ADMIRALS:

Bobby & Ann Archer   *Ann's Southern Jewel* (Bluewater)

BB Customs

The Fuchs Family

In Honor of Capt. Welton & Betty Jetton who sponsored the LaGasses for membership in 1995

CAPTAINS:

Tim & Paula Balakas   *Playen II*

Cliff & Katie Buck   *License to Chill*

Marine Supply Company

Kay & Chuck Cook   *Twin Angel*

Kellie & Ted Cortese   *Kellie Bears*

Andy & Marion Crenshaw   *Totally Hip*

Mike & Dianne Dolan's Accent Countertops

—list of CAPTAIN's contingent continued next page

W.C. Ellis Ironworks, Boat Machine Shop Est. 1862

In Memory of Tom and Sis Lee

Tom Lewis & Cathy Schanzer   *Caritas*

Sylvester's Automotive Foreign and Domestic

Ron Oliver & Jane Walker

David Earl Patterson

Phil & Athala Pierini   *Good News*

Victor & Suzette Quarles   *Jubilee III*

Outdoors, Inc. Annual Canoe & Kayak Race

Jake & Terry Saunders   *Knot Yet*

Bob & Laura Schwartz

Ham & Katherine Smythe   *Sapphire & Bombay Duck*

Chip Sneed & Donna Boyce   *Chip's Ahoy*

Cheryl & Garland Sullivan   *Apache*